Edward Ely Dunbar

The Romance of the Age

The Discovery of Gold in California

Edward Ely Dunbar

The Romance of the Age
The Discovery of Gold in California

ISBN/EAN: 9783337048259

Printed in Europe, USA, Canada, Australia, Japan

Cover: Foto ©ninafisch / pixelio.de

More available books at **www.hansebooks.com**

JOHN A. SUTTER.

THE ROMANCE OF THE AGE;

OR, THE DISCOVERY OF GOLD

IN CALIFORNIA.

BY

EDWARD E. DUNBAR.

NEW YORK:
D. APPLETON AND COMPANY.
443 & 445 BROADWAY.
1867.

Entered according to Act of Congress, in the year 1867, by
D. APPLETON & CO.,
in the Clerk's Office of the District Court of the United States for the Southern District of New York.

TO THE

MEMBERS OF THE TRAVELLERS' CLUB

OF THE

CITY OF NEW YORK,

This Work

IS RESPECTFULLY DEDICATED BY

THE AUTHOR.

CONTENTS.

	Page
INTRODUCTION,	7
EARLY HISTORY OF SUTTER,	11
REMARKABLE COMBINATION OF EVENTS ATTENDING THE DISCOVERY OF GOLD,	26
ATTEMPT OF THE AMERICANS TO ACQUIRE CALIFORNIA—THE BEAR FLAG,	29
THE MEXICAN WAR—THE AMERICANS TAKE POSSESSION OF CALIFORNIA,	37
CALIFORNIA CONQUERED,	41
THE MORMONS,	42
THE END OF THE MEXICAN WAR—ACQUISITION OF CALIFORNIA,	47
ESTABLISHMENT OF THE PACIFIC MAIL LINE OF STEAMERS,	48
THE TRIP OF THE FIRST PASSENGERS FROM NEW YORK TO SAN FRANCISCO BY STEAMER,	55

CONTENTS.

	Page
No Positive Knowledge of the Existence of Gold in California, previous to its Discovery,	92
Sutter's Condition in 1848,	103
Marshall,	105
Location of the Saw-Mill,	106
Discovery of the Gold,	107
The Discovery of Gold becomes Public,	113
Consequences of the Discovery to Marshall,	118
Consequences of the Discovery to Sutter,	124

THE ROMANCE OF THE AGE;

OR,

THE DISCOVERY OF GOLD IN CALIFORNIA.

Somebody has said that history is an incorrigible liar. This remark is doubtless true in a greater or less degree, as applied to contemporaneous history, which, being written amid the excitement of events as they occur, and under the influence of selfish motives, passion or prejudice, can only be relied upon for its record of facts, that cannot be perverted, and from which false conclusions cannot be deduced.

The discovery of a New World by Columbus is one of those great events respecting which there can be no mistake. It will forever loom up a towering headland on the shore of Time, to mark the progress of the world. But Columbus, in his day, was misunderstood, undervalued, maligned, and finally he sank into his grave a persecuted, heart-broken man. The envy, jealousy, ignorance, and selfishness of small and depraved minds, all worked together to hurl the great discoverer from the lofty position he had attained. It is only by filtering facts down through the crevices of ages that great truths are realized, and time alone can work out a due appreciation of great men and the great events they represent.

Three hundred and seventy-five years have elapsed since Columbus discovered America. The inspiration, the genius, the heroism of the great discoverer are more clearly discerned and vastly better appreciated by the present generation than they were by his own; and the magnitude and importance of the event itself are more thoroughly realized as time rolls on and develops the momentous results.

So with the discovery of gold in California. We who are living witnesses of the great event fail to recognize its importance. In the excitement of the time, in our familiarity with the men and circumstances connected with the discovery, we, the first greedy, selfish, unreflecting participants in the results, pass away, and leave it for future generations to appreciate the occurrence and properly estimate its effect on the world at large. As yet no attempt to give a connected account of the wonderful discovery of gold in California, with the remarkable combination of events attending the occurrence, has been made. In my present effort I propose simply to rescue certain important facts from oblivion, hoping they may prove an instructive, entertaining record at the present time, and of use to the future historian. Many of the facts stated are of my own personal knowledge; others are gathered from living witnesses, participators in the scenes described, and who, a few years hence, will have passed from the stage of action, thus sealing forever to human investigation the only reliable source of information so interesting and important.

It is true that the discovery of gold in California was accidental. This event had not the *éclat* of national preparation or government patronage, such, for instance, as attended the departure of the first expedition down the western coast of Africa, under Antonio Gonçalves, in the time of Henry, Prince of Portugal, or that of Columbus from Spain. The great discovery in California was not the result of any foreknowledge, preparation, or plan. Though it flashed upon the world like an unexpected, unpredicted meteor, the occurrence was, in reality, the result of a combination of circumstances as remarkable, perhaps, as ever preceded or led to any of the great events that mark the history of the world.

No religious, political, or scientific organization could claim any direct agency in the great discovery, and none could command its exclusive benefits. This event, so far beyond the reach of any one selfish interest, so world-wide in its practical results, was at last accidentally wrought out by natural means, as humble and obscure as those which gave to the world the manger-born founder of Christianity.

Nearly all great discoveries are accidental, and sometimes the most trivial circumstances lead to the greatest. It is said the principle of gravitation was thumped into the brain of Newton by a pippin, which fell upon the cranium of the philosopher as he lay musing under the shade of the parent tree. The discovery of America, even, by Columbus, was accidental, for history says that he sailed to discover a nearer passage to the East Indies, and in due course he ran against a continent. So Marshall, the humble employé or associate of the pioneer Sutter, while digging a saw-mill race away in the remote and wild regions of California, discovered the shining particles of life's great lubricator.

SUTTER.

In the history of the discovery of gold in California, no one stands forth so prominent as JOHN A. SUTTER. This distinguished pioneer is, in reality, the hero of the grandest history of modern times.

Born of Swiss parents in Baden, February 28th, 1803, reared and educated in that city, Sutter entered the military service of France as captain, where he remained until thirty years of age. At this period, yielding to his pioneer impulses, the young adventurer embarked for New York, where he arrived July, 1834.

Captain Sutter's object in coming to the United States was to select a locality and prepare the way for a colony of Swiss—his countrymen. He at once proceeded to the unexplored territory west of the Mississippi, and selected the region of St. Charles, in Missouri, as a proper location for his proposed colony. But this enterprise was ultimately abandoned, from the fact that the vessel containing the effects upon which Sutter relied to accomplish his colonizing project, was sunk in the Mississippi, and proved a total loss.

After sojourning for a time in St. Charles, where he declared his intention to become an American citizen, Captain Sutter made a journey of exploration to New Mexico, and returned to Missouri in 1836. When in New Mexico, he met with hunters and trappers who had traversed Upper California, and who described to him the beautiful sunlit valleys, verdure-covered hills, and magnificent mountains of that remarkable land. These accounts so charmed Sutter, that he resolved to make California the field of his future adventures.

The only way of reaching the Pacific coast at this period was to accompany the trapping expeditions of the American and English fur companies. In the month of March, 1838, Sutter joined Captain Tripp, of the American Fur Company, and travelled with his party to their rendezvous in the Rocky Mountains. From thence, with six horsemen, he crossed the mountains, and after encountering the inevitable hardships and dangers of the journey, the party arrived at Fort Vancouver.

There was then no land route from Oregon to California that could be travelled in winter; and as there was a vessel belonging to the Hudson Bay Company ready to sail for the Sandwich Islands, Sutter took passage in this vessel hoping to find a conveyance to California from Honolulu.

On reaching the Sandwich Islands he found no available means of passage to California, and after sojourning there five months, he concluded to ship as supercargo on board an English vessel, chartered by an American, and bound for

Sitka. Having disposed of the cargo at Sitka, Sutter sailed, according to instructions, down the Pacific coast. Encountering heavy gales, the vessel was driven into the Bay of San Francisco in a distressed condition. They came to anchor opposite Yerba Buena, now San Francisco, on the 2d of July, 1839.

The vessel was soon boarded by an officer, who ordered the captain to leave for Monterey, the port of entry, ninety miles south. Permission was obtained to remain forty-eight hours for supplies. On arriving in Monterey, Sutter, having dispatched the vessel back to her owners in the Sandwich Islands, waited upon Alvarado, the Mexican governor, and communicated to him his desire to occupy and colonize a section of country on the Sacramento River.

The governor warmly approved of this plan, as he was desirous that the Sacramento country, inhabited only by wild and hostile Indians, should be subdued and settled. Alvarado readily gave Sutter a passport, with power to explore and occupy any territory he should think suitable for his colony, and stated that if he returned within one year, he should be acknowledged as a citizen, and receive a grant for such lands as he might solicit.

Captain Sutter, thus empowered, returned to Yerba Buena, a settlement then containing scarcely fifty inhabitants. He chartered a schooner and several small boats of the firm of Leese, Spear & Hinckly, three American traders who had been located at this point several years. Jacob P. Leese was the first American settler in Yerba Buena. He settled in that place in 1833, having emigrated from Pennsylvania; and as a true and enterprising pioneer, he stands prominent in the history of California at that period.

Captain Sutter could find no one at Yerba Buena who had ever seen the Sacramento River, or who could guide him to its mouth. They only knew that a large stream emptied into one of the connecting bays lying in a northerly direction. Sutter resolved, however, to start with his company, consisting of ten whites—frontiersmen of American, Irish, and German birth—and eight Kanakas given to him by the King of the Sandwich Islands. Passing through San Francisco and Suisun Bays, they found, after eight days' search, the mouth of the Sacramento. Ascending this river to a point ten miles below the present site of Sacramento City, they encountered a party of two hundred Indian warriors, who exhibited every mark of hostility. Fortunately, several of these Indians understood Spanish, and Captain Sutter soon soothed them with assurances that there were no Mexicans—against whom they were particularly exasperated and hostile—in his party. He explained to them that he came to settle in their country and trade; exhibited his agricultural implements and commodities of traffic, which he had prepared for the purpose, and set forth the advantages of a treaty. Pleased with these kindly and peaceful demonstrations, the Indians became pacified, and the expedition was permitted to proceed, accompanied by the two Indians who spoke Spanish, and who guided them to the mouth of the Feather River.

Having ascended this river some distance, several of the party became alarmed at the surrounding dangers, and insisted on returning. Sutter consented to return to the mouth of the American River, where, on the 16th of August,

1839, he caused his effects to be landed on the south bank, a short distance from its junction with the Sacramento, where the city of Sacramento now stands. Having landed his effects, Captain Sutter informed his party, that any feeling disaffected were at liberty to leave, he being resolved to remain at all hazards. But three of the party—whites—determined to go, and being put in possession of the schooner, to be returned to her owners at Yerba Buena, they left on that day. Captain Sutter fixed upon this locality as his permanent headquarters, and he soon commenced to build the fort, afterward famous as SUTTER'S FORT.

This, in brief, is the history of Captain Sutter up to the period when he made his final lodgment in California. We find him located at last in the region of country for which the aspirations of years of youth and manhood had caused him to search, and which five years of actual wandering had enabled him to reach. Our interest in the pioneer increases. Little did Sutter think, when he located in that wild, remote region, that he was to be one of the main instruments in suddenly creating a magnificent empire. When we reflect on the innumerable hardships and dangers through which Sutter must have passed, by land and by sea, during those years of determined effort to locate in the Sacramento country—a region far, far removed from civilization, and as little known, perhaps, as any on the face of the earth—we are almost forced to believe that he was moved by an inspiration of great things to come.

There is something extravagantly romantic as well as ludicrous in the situation of this blue-eyed Swiss, when he located in the Sacramento valley. His companions were six wandering whites, of various nationalities, and eight Kanakas, of whom, the latter, ever faithful, constituted what he called his body-guard. These fourteen companions made up his colony, and his army, by means of which he was to hold his ground, and subdue and colonize a district of country entirely unknown, and inhabited only by wild and roving bands of hostile Indians. This portion of Upper California, though fair to look upon, was peculiarly solitary and uninviting in its isolation and remoteness from civilization. There was not even one of those cattle-ranches, which dotted the coast at long intervals, nearer to Sutter's locality than Suisun and Martinez, below the mouth of the Sacramento.

The Indians of the Sacramento were known as "Diggers." The efforts of the Jesuit Fathers, so extensive on this continent, and so beneficial to the wild Indians, wherever missions were established among them, never reached the wretched aborigines of the Sacramento country. The valley of the Sacramento had not yet become the pathway of emigrants from the East, and no civilized human being lived in this primitive and solitary region, or roamed over it, if we except a few trappers of the Hudson Bay Company.

Every human heart has its own secret history. None but the true pioneer—the loyal sympathizer with Nature—can conceive what Captain Sutter saw inviting at that time in this remote and secluded spot, or what was his leading motive in locating there to establish, it would seem, a frontier community of his own. It was no doubt from a pure love of this kind of life, an irrepressible desire to lead the van of civilization. It would appear that even at this early period, the bright glimmering of the star of empire in the western heavens revealed itself to his pioneer spirit, which, catching the inspiration, impelled him on and on toward the setting sun, until he reached the utmost confines of the Western Hemisphere, where he cast his lot, to prepare the way for and await civilization. Its first footsteps had not been seen or heard when Sutter located there. Years passed, and a few came stealing over the border; then more; then a firm, solid tramp of masses was heard; and then rushed headlong a human deluge, that overwhelmed our bold pioneer, and it may be said that he has been whirling in its vortex ever since.

Born and reared in the atmosphere of royalty and refined society in Europe, with a liberal military education, gentle and polished manners, and of unbounded liberality of heart, we find Captain Sutter successfully planting his little colony in the secluded and hostile Sacramento valley.

At first this little colony encountered serious difficulties with the Indians, and the increase of the settlement was slow. The tide of American emigration was entirely to Oregon, from whence a few stragglers occasionally found their way to Sutter's colony. In the fall of 1839 there was an accession of eight white men, and in August, 1840, five of those who had crossed the Rocky Mountains with Sutter, and whom he had left in Oregon, joined him. During the fall of this year the Mokelumne Indians, with other tribes, became so troublesome that Sutter and his little band waged open warfare against them, and, after a severe but short campaign, they were beaten on every side and forced to keep the peace. Other bands of Indians organized many secret expeditious to destroy the colony, but by force and strict vigilance these machinations were finally frustrated, and Sutter soon conquered the entire Sacramento and part of the San Joaquin valley, bringing into willing subjection many of those who had been his fiercest enemies. In due time he taught them a certain degree of civilization. He established a police among themselves; of some he formed a body of uniformed soldiers, and many of these became good artillerists and riflemen. Others were required to learn several of the mechanical trades, and a large number were made to cultivate the soil, herd cattle, etc., etc. In due time they built what afterward became famous as Sutter's Fort. Several cannon were mounted, and an abundant supply of small-arms and ammunition was acquired. In the subsequent military history of Upper California, Sutter and his Indians became a power in the land.

In course of time, progress and prosperity attended the colony. Sutter sent hides to Yerba Buena, furnished the Hudson Bay Company and wandering trappers with supplies, receiving in exchange their furs. Emigrants who sought work were employed as mechanics or tillers of the soil.

In June, 1841, Sutter visited Monterey, the capital of the province, where he was declared a Mexican citizen, and received from Governor Alvarado a grant of the land upon which he had located—eleven leagues—under the title of "New Helvetia." Alvarado also gave him a commission as the *representante del gobierno en las fronteras del norte, y encargado de la justicia.*

SUTTER'S FORT.

Returning to his colony, Sutter was shortly after visited by Captain Ringgold, of the United States Exploring Expedition, under Commander Wilkes. About the same time Mr. Alexander Rotchoff, Governor of the Russian Possessions, known as "Ross & Bodega," situated on the coast near the entrance of San Francisco Bay, visited Sutter and offered to sell him all those possessions. The negotiation was finally concluded, and Sutter came into possession of all the real and personal property, in the latter of which were two thousand cattle, one thousand horses, fifty mules, and two thousand five hundred sheep. This increase of Sutter's resources, together with the natural increase of his stock and other property at New Helvetia, enabled him the more rapidly to advance his settlement and improvements.

In the year 1844 Sutter petitioned Governor Manuel Micheltorena for the grant or purchase of the *sobrante*, or surplus over the first eleven leagues of the land within the bounds of the survey accompanying the Alvarado grant. In February, 1845, Micheltorena complied with Sutter's petition, partly on account of military services rendered the State in suppressing the Castro rebellion.

About this period, (1844) small bodies of emigrants began to find their way to California direct from the States, striking Sutter's Fort, the first settlement after crossing the mountains. Year by year these emigrants increased in numbers, till the discovery of gold, when they were counted by thousands and tens of thousands.

It is here that the value of Sutter's settlement, and the generous qualities of the man, became strikingly apparent. No weary, travel-worn and destitute emigrant ever reached Sutter's Fort, who was not supplied with every necessary, and sent on his way rejoicing. The cry of distress never came over the mountains from any party of emigrants, however large, but what it received the immediate attention of the noble-hearted Sutter. Cattle, in droves, with the necessary number of horses and Indians, were at once dispatched to supply the broken-down, starving emigrants, and bring them safely in.

The following incident was related to me by Sutter. It exhibits something of the terrible hardships to which emigrants to the Pacific shores were then exposed.

A solitary emigrant was just able to reach Sutter's Fort, and report his companions some distance back in the desert country, dying of starvation. Sutter immediately caused a number of his best mules to be packed with supplies, and dispatched under the guidance of the messenger and two Indians. They arrived among the starving emigrants in time to save most of them, but just as they were about to move forward, another party of famishing emigrants unexpectedly arrived. In their frenzy they seized upon all that remained of the supplies sent by Sutter, killed his mules and ate them; then they killed the two Indians and ate them. Said Sutter with much feeling: "They eat my fine Indians all up." After eating numbers of their companions as they fell exhausted and lifeless, the remaining portion of these wretched emigrants finally arrived at Sutter's Fort, where they were supplied with all the necessaries of life, and maintained until their health and strength were restored. Year after year Sutter exercised this munificent liberality and kindness, never looking for or accepting any reward.

REMARKABLE COMBINATION OF EVENTS ATTENDING THE DISCOVERY OF GOLD.

We will now leave Sutter in his adventurous, prosperous career, to set forth that remarkable combination of events preceding the discovery of gold in California, and which has a very important bearing on the realization of the fact itself.

Mankind, under the influence of superstitious vagaries, are prone to attribute remarkable coincidences and occurrences they do not comprehend to a supernatural agency. In the present instance it would add so much to the piquancy and romantic interest of the history, by casting upon it the fitful glimmer of supernaturalism, that the historian is sorely tempted to be less clear in his explanation of the natural causes of the events chronicled.

It must be acknowledged that the precise working of events in cycles, all tending with undeviating precision to the discovery of gold in California, and the rapid development of its results, is remarkable and in the highest degree interesting. The superstitious would characterize this—to use the mild term of the age—as a special providence, which means that Nature will go out of her way in all things, from serving an old lady with a cup of tea, to the creation or destruction of an empire.

This superstitious belief drags God and His laws down to the fallible standard of sinful man. It affords the excuse for ten great crimes where it incites to one small virtue. It underlies all the prevailing systems of religion, and it engenders the several degrees of fanaticism alike in Thug, Dervish, Jesuit, and Puritan; and so long as it rules the world as at present, the pure and simple religion of Jesus Christ can never attain.

Omnipotent Power, in administering the whole law, which is the law of progressive good, cannot deviate to the right hand or to the left. This makes providences general, and not special, as applied by the superstitious masses.

At the time gold was discovered in California, that country was practically a *terra incognita* to the whole world. It must be said, however, that the hour had come. Events were big in the womb of time. The greedy eye of the commercial world was beginning to turn toward that fair land. Ocean steam-navigation and the electric telegraph had just become established successes, and there was that natural tendency to explore for new fields which increased populations and augmented facilities of great importance and variety would naturally induce, particularly in the American and English nations.

Subsequent to 1844, the tendency of events in California was such as to render the possession of that territory a political necessity to the United States. Our omnipresent rival, England, was looking to that coast with wistful eyes. It was known that Mexico was about to give one McNamara, an Irish Catholic priest, immense land grants, such as would include the best portions of Upper California; and these land grants McNamara had stipulated to place under a British protectorate.

At this period (1844) there were located in

California but few Americans. Those most prominent were Thomas O. Larkin, in Monterey; Leese, Spear & Hinckley, in Yerba Buena; George Yount, in Sonoma; and Bidwell, Reading & Hensly, in other parts of the territory. But now others came straggling into the country from Oregon and from over the Sierra Nevada, while others landed on the coast. Early in 1846, the Americans in California numbered about 200, mostly able-bodied men, and who in their activity, enterprise, and audacity, constituted quite a formidable element in this sparsely inhabited region. The population of California at this time was 6,000 Mexicans and 200,000 Indians.

ATTEMPT OF THE AMERICANS TO ACQUIRE CALIFORNIA.—THE BEAR FLAG.

We now come to a period in the history of California that has never been made clear, and respecting which there are conflicting statements and opinions. The following facts were obtained by careful inquiry of intelligent parties who lived in California during the period mentioned, and who participated in the scenes narrated.

The native Californians appear to have entertained no very strong affection for their own government, or rather, they felt that under the influences at work they would inevitably, and at no distant period, become a dismembered branch of the Mexican nation; and the matter was finally narrowed down to this contested point, namely, whether this state surgery should be performed by Americans or English, the real struggle being between these two nationalities.

In the northern part of the territory, such native Californians as the Vallejos, Castros, etc., with the old American settlers, Leese, Larkin, and others, sympathized with the United States, and desired annexation to the American republic. In the south, Pio Pico, then governor of the territory, and other prominent native Californians, with James Alexander Forbes, the English consul, who settled in Santa Clara in 1828, were exerting themselves to bring the country under English domination by means of the McNamara papers, or other pretexts.

This was the state of affairs for two or three

years previous to the Mexican War. For some months before the news that hostilities between the United States and Mexico had commenced reached California, the belief that such an event would certainly occur, was universal throughout the territory. This quickened the impulses of all parties, and stimulated the two rivals—the American and English—in their efforts to be the first to obtain a permanent hold of the country.

The United States Government had sent Colonel Fremont to the Pacific on an exploring expedition. Colonel Fremont had passed through California, and was on his way to Oregon, when, in March, 1846, Lieutenant Gillespie, of the United States marine service, was sent from Washington with dispatches to Colonel Fremont. Lieutenant Gillespie went across Mexico to Mazatlan, and from thence by sea to California. He finally overtook Fremont early in June, 1846, a short distance on the road to Oregon, and communicated to him the purport of his dispatches, they having been committed to memory and the papers destroyed before he entered Mexico. What these instructions authorized Colonel Fremont to do has never been promulgated, but it is said they directed him to remain in California, and hold himself in readiness to coöperate with the United States fleet, in case war with Mexico should occur.

Fremont immediately returned to California, and camped a short time on Feather River, and then took up his headquarters at Sutter's Fort. A few days after, on Sunday, June 14th, 1846, a party of fourteen Americans, under no apparent command, appeared in Sonoma, captured the place, raised the Bear flag, proclaimed the independence of California, and carried off to Fremont's quarters as prisoners four prominent citizens, namely, the two Vallejos, J. P. Leese, and Colonel Prudhon. On the consummation of these achievements, one Merritt was elected captain.

This was a rough party of revolutionists, and the manner in which they improvised the famous Bear flag, shows upon what slender means nations and kingdoms are sometimes started. From an estimable old lady they obtained a fragmentary portion of her white skirt, on which they painted what was intended to represent a grizzly bear, but not being artistic in their work, it was difficult to determine what kind of an animal they had selected as the emblem of the new natiouality; so the Mexicans, with their usual happy faculty on such occasions, called it the "*Bandera Colchis,*" or "Hog Flag." This flag now ornaments the rooms of the Pioneer Society in San Francisco.

On the 18th of June, 1846, William B. Ide, a native of New England, who had emigrated to California the year previous, issued a proclamation as commander-in-chief of the fortress of Sonoma. This proclamation declared the purpose to overthrow the existing government, and establish in its place the republican form. The proclamation particularly requested the people to remain at peace, and follow their usual occupations, while the change that was to bring every imaginable blessing to the country took place.

General Castro now proposed to attack the feebly-manned post at Sonoma, but he was frustrated by a rapid movement of Fremont, who, on the 4th of July, 1846, called a meeting of Americans at Sonoma; and this assembly, act-ing under his advice, proclaimed the independence of the country, appointed Fremont Governor, and declared war against Mexico.

During these proceedings at Sonoma, a flag with one star floated over the headquarters of Fremont at Sutter's Fort. The meaning of this lone-star flag no one seems to have understood, nor, in fact, does it appear to be known to this day precisely what end the several parties engaged in these military movements (under the direction, it was supposed, of Fremont) had in view. The people of Northern California appeared at first to take no very decided stand against the raising of the Bear flag, and the proclamation of the independence of California. They were very much incensed, however, by the capture and imprisonment of four of their most prominent citizens; and they allege that when Colonel Fremont appeared in the country and took a leading part, his course was so indiscreet as to create an antagonism to American interests, and provoke the warlike opposition which subsequently manifested itself among the native inhabitants, when otherwise there would have been only friendship.

This allegation would appear to be sustained from the fact that Governor Pio Pico, the head of the anti-American party in Southern California, speedily and adroitly seized upon the act of the Americans in capturing Sonoma, to inflame the minds of the people against foreigners of the United States of America, as appears by the following extract from a communication addressed by Governor Pico to Thomas O. Larkin, Esq., United States consul, and dated Santa Barbara, June 29, 1846:

"The undersigned, constitutional Governor of the Department of the Californias, has the deep mortification to make known to Mr. Thomas O. Larkin, consul of the United States of North America, that he has been greatly surprised in being notified by official communications of the general commandancia of this Department, and the prefectura of the second district, that a multitude of foreigners of the United States of America have invaded that frontier, taken possession of the fortified town of Sonoma, treacherously making prisoners of the military commandante, Don Mariano G. Vallejo, Lieut.-Colonel Victor Prudhon, Captain

Salvador Vallejo, and Mr. Jacob P. Leese; and likewise have stolen the property of these individuals.

"The undersigned can do no less than make known to the consul of the United States that acts so alarming have caused very great grief.

"Until the present the department governor is wanting the least positive information that would give him to understand of a declaration of war between the United States and Mexico; and, without such information, he judges the course pursued at Sonoma the most atrocious and infamous that can be imagined, so much so that the like is not seen among barbarians."

It was believed by many in California that those directing the movements of the Bear-flag party intended to establish an independent republic.

I simply state these historical facts, without entering into further details, or giving any opinion as to the merits of the controversy, which at one time was carried on with great bitterness. It may be that the action of the censured party was dictated by a desire to secure the country to the United States before England could raise any claim.

THE MEXICAN WAR.—THE AMERICANS TAKE POSSESSION OF CALIFORNIA.

Pending these movements, and just as Fremont, with his company, had started for the coast to confront Castro, and act on the aggressive generally, he was suddenly brought to a stand by the astounding intelligence that Commodore Sloat had arrived at Monterey, and that on the 7th of July, 1846, he had raised the American flag and taken possession of the place; also, that, by command of Commodore Sloat, Commander Montgomery, of the United States sloop-of-war Portsmouth, then lying in San Francisco Bay, had, on the 8th of July, taken possession of Yerba Buena, and raised the American flag on the plaza. This of course settled the business for all parties. The Mexican flag and the Bear flag were lowered, and in due time, *nolens volens*, all acquiesced in the flying of the Stars and Stripes.

The accounts, even among Californians, respecting the date on which the American flag was raised at Monterey, the circumstances attending this important event, and the degree of responsibility assumed by Commodore Sloat, are somewhat conflicting.

By the kindness of L. W. Sloat, Jr., Esq., who was on board the Savannah, commanded by his father, I have been furnished with the following extracts from the ship's log :

"*U. S. Frigate Savannah, Commodore* SLOAT.
MAZATLAN, MEXICO, *May* 31, 1846.

"Received report of General Taylor's victory over the Mexicans on the 8th and 9th of May, on the north bank of the Rio Bravo.

"June 5th. News of General Taylor's victories confirmed—of his taking possession of Matamoras the 18th of May, received.

"June 7th. Lieutenant Trapin performed divine service. News received of the blockade of Vera Cruz by the American squadron. At 2 P. M. got under way for Monterey, California.

"July 1st. Stood into the harbor of Monterey, and came to anchor at 4 P. M. in front of the town, about one-quarter of a mile from the fort, which bore by compass N. W. The captain of the port, accompanied by Mr. Hartwell, attached to the Custom-House, called. Cyane and Levant in port.

"July 2d. Thomas O. Larkin, Esq., United States consul, made a long call, and on leaving was saluted with nine guns.

"July 3d. Called upon the authorities.

"July 4th. Ship dressed and salutes fired.

"July 5th. Lieutenant Trapin performed divine service.

"July 6th. Mr. Larkin spent the day on board preparing proclamations, etc., for taking possession of California to-morrow.

"July 7th. Seven A. M., landing forces. Took possession; hoisted flag.

"July 15th. United States frigate Congress, Commodore Stockton, arrived from Honolulu. Whilst in the offing, saluted the flag with thirteen guns, which was returned. R. M. Price and Dr. Gilchrist appointed alcaldes of Monterey.

"July 27th. Gave up the command of the squadron to Commodore Stockton to-day, and turned over to him the papers appertaining thereto.

"July 29th. Sailed in Levant for Mazatlan and Panama."

These extracts from Commodore Sloat's log settle all questions as to dates, and they prove the fact that, though the commodore had heard of the commencement of hostilities on the Rio Grande, he sailed from Mazatlan for California, took possession of the country, and raised the American flag on his own responsibility.

These decisive steps on the part of Commodore Sloat were not taken a moment too soon, as on the 14th of July the British man-of-war Collingwood, Sir George Seymour commanding, arrived at Monterey, and, to his utter amazement, he saw the American flag flying from the Mexican fort, and the town in possession of the Americans.

Sir George Seymour informed Commodore Sloat that he could salute his ship, but he could not salute the American flag ashore, for he had come to do the same thing; that is, he had come to take possession of that portion of the country and raise the English flag. This was to have been done on the strength of the McNamara papers, which the English commander believed had been executed and delivered. It is said these papers subsequently fell into the hands of one of the United States army officers in Southern California.

CALIFORNIA CONQUERED.

Commodore Stockton, on assuming command of the squadron, immediately instituted bold and vigorous measures for the subjugation of the territory. All his available force for land operations was three hundred and fifty men—sailors and marines. But so rapid and skilful were Stockton's movements, and so efficient was the coöperation of Fremont with his small troop, that California was effectually conquered in January, 1847.

During all this period the people of the United States were ignorant of what was transpiring in California, and *vice versa*. But the action of Commodore Sloat in raising the American flag in California, and that of Commodore Stockton in conquering the territory, did but anticipate the wishes of the United States Government, which had in June, 1846, dispatched General Kearney across the country from Fort Leavenworth, at the head of sixteen hundred men, with orders to conquer California, and when conquered, to assume the governorship of the territory. General Kearney arrived in California *via* San Pasqual with greatly diminished forces, December, 1846, a few weeks before active military operations in that region ceased.

The United States Government had also dispatched a regiment of volunteers from New York *via* Cape Horn, under Colonel J. D. Stevenson, September, 1846. This regiment arrived in San Francisco, March, 1847, and in detached bodies it performed garrison duty throughout the conquered territory, until peace was declared.

THE MORMONS.

The Mormon movement should here be explained, as furnishing a singular coincidence in connection with affairs in California at this period, not omitting the serio-comic end of Mormon hopes brought about by the war with Mexico.

The exodus of the Mormons from Nauvoo took place in the early part of 1846. It is a well-known fact that this singular people had become so obnoxious in the West, that their presence in any great numbers was not tolerated. In February, 1846, sixteen hundred men, women, and children, constituting the main body of the sect inhabiting Nauvoo City, started with their movable effects for the Pacific, shaking the dust from their feet, and hurling anathemas loud and deep against the people and institutions of the United States. Those who remained in Nauvoo were soon forced to follow the main body, and the city with its temple finally became a heap of ruins. The destination of the polygamists was California, some part of which territory, especially that bordering on San Francisco Bay, they proposed to acquire from Mexico.

Simultaneously with the movement of the main body of the Mormons from Nauvoo City, some two hundred of the sect, including several of their prominent leaders, purchased the ship Brooklyn, and sailed from New York, January, 1846, for San Francisco Bay, where they arrived July 31st, but twenty-three days after Commander Montgomery had taken possession of the place and raised the American flag.

It was a fine, brilliant California day, that

on which the Mormon-freighted ship Brooklyn passed through the Golden Gate and entered San Francisco Bay. The long-wished-for haven was gained at last. What a magnificent harbor! What a fine country! And all that virgin territory awaiting in silence and peace the coming of the latter-day saints. These, as may be imagined, weary of their long and tedious voyage, were eager to set foot on the promised land flowing with milk and honey, where, free from persecution, like the Pilgrims of old, they could worship God after their own fashion, and where polygamous institutions were to rise in all their loveliness, beauty, and grandeur.

The Brooklyn sailed majestically into the bay, her decks crowded with impatient human beings, when, on coming opposite the town, one of the leaders was observed to shade his eyes and gaze anxiously ashore. Suddenly his countenance became ghastly, and, pointing to our national emblem, which floated over the plaza in all its beauty and glory, he exclaimed, "*By God! there is that damned American flag!*"

These Mormons had left the United States several months before the commencement of the war with Mexico, and the sight of our flag floating over the plaza of Yerba Buena was the first intimation they had of that event and its consequences. An express was immediately sent off to meet the main body of Mormons coming overland. This Mormon host had pursued their toilsome march westward to the 20th July, 1846, when, from the Wasatch Mountains, they beheld the placid waters of Salt Lake, gilded by the beams of the setting sun. On the 24th, just one week previous to the arrival of the Brooklyn in San Francisco Bay, the entire body of Mormons, with the High Council and the President, reached the valley and camped to recruit their exhausted strength. Here they were met by the express from the Brooklyn, with the astounding intelligence that the Americans had taken possession of California, and that the project of finding a resting-place on the Pacific shore must be abandoned. After a brief deliberation, they determined to remain where they were. This conclusion was the more readily reached, as the land was good, and the isolated location offered great advantages. Planting commenced immediately, and measures were at once taken to build their seat of empire, now known as Salt Lake City. This explains the settlement of the Mormons in Utah.

But this people did not long remain unmolested in their new locality, for they were speedily called upon and compelled by the United States Government to furnish a battalion to serve in California. Under officers of the United States Army, this battalion was marched forthwith to that territory, and it must be said that it performed good and faithful service until the end of the war.

The Brooklyn party, disappointed and dispirited, soon quarrelled among themselves, and finally dispersed. Some remained in Yerba Buena, while others settled in the Sacramento Valley, and yet a company of others went to San Bernardino, in the southern part of the State, and there formed a settlement.

Several of these prominent Mormons who had come so far to get beyond the reach of the American flag, and who remained in California, eschewed Mormonism, contented themselves with the dual blessedness of the Gentiles, amassed wealth, and became good and influential citizens. When the great rebellion broke out, instances of boisterous loyalty among them occurred, and it was refreshing to behold the intense affection they manifested for the old flag, and their liberal contributions to sustain its glory. Thus runs the world. Circumstances alter cases. We may live to see the day when those same parties will deem it expedient to curse the American flag as heartily as ever.

THE END OF THE MEXICAN WAR.—ACQUISITION OF CALIFORNIA.

The arrival of the several military bodies that have been mentioned, of the Mormons and other emigrants who found their way over the Snowy Mountains and from Oregon, considerably augmented the white population of California in the years 1846–'47. The number of white emigrants—soldiers and civilians—settled throughout California in the early part of 1848, when the gold was discovered, may be estimated at two thousand. While active hostilities continued in Central Mexico, peace and order, under American rule, were maintained throughout California.

It will be perceived that the Mexican War had an immediate and direct effect on the destiny of California—more so, perhaps, than on that of any other portion of Mexican territory; and it precipitated the development of the great wealth discovered at that period. The war commenced in April, 1846, and terminated by a treaty of peace in which, for a trifling consideration, we came into quiet possession of the entire territory, with New Mexico, February 2, 1848, the very day on which gold was discovered in California!

ESTABLISHMENT OF THE PACIFIC MAIL LINE OF STEAMERS.

There is still another event which I will narrate, as one of the singular coincidences, and as having a highly important bearing on the rapid development of the discovery of gold in California, namely, the establishment of the Pacific mail line of steamers, in connection with

Sloo's line to New Orleans and Chagres. Many, doubtless, believe that these lines of steamers were called into existence by the discovery of gold in California. The great discovery had nothing to do with originating these enterprises.

The idea of an American line of mail-steamers from Panama up the Pacific coast, touching at several Mexican ports and terminating at Astoria, Oregon, is said to have originated with one J. M. Shively, a plain sort of man, who, at an early day, drifted from Massachusetts or Connecticut, across the continent, and finally located at Astoria, of which place he was appointed postmaster. Shively returned to the United States in 1845, and when in Washington, it is said, he suggested this line of steamers.

At this time the controversy between the United States and Great Britain, respecting the Northwestern boundary, had become a very exciting topic. Our Government was exceedingly anxious to turn emigration into Oregon, and it is possible that Shively's idea of a line of steamers from Panama up the Pacific coast, may have been regarded favorably in Washington.

Whether this be true or not, President Polk, in the latter part of 1845, took decided measures to establish a means of conveyance to Oregon, that should be available to emigrants. In furtherance of this project, the President invited Mr. J. M. Woodward, of New York, to visit Washington, and assist him with his information and counsels.

Mr. Woodward was then engaged in the Baltic trade, and he had frequent and large consignments of emigrants from Norway, Sweden, Denmark, and Prussia. He at once complied with the President's request. After several conferences with this high official, and some weeks spent in obtaining all the information possible on the subject, Mr. Woodward presented the following plan, namely:

To prepare and send out a number of small boats, sufficient to take an entire shipment of emigrants and their baggage from the vessels, on their arrival at Chagres, and proceed up the Chagres River as far as Cruces; from thence by pack-mules across the Isthmus of Panama, whence they were to embark on board sailing or steam vessels for Oregon. This plan was accompanied by the requisite estimates for its accomplishment, and the whole was submitted in the shape of a report to the President. He signified his hearty approval of the plan proposed, and by his direction, immediate steps were taken to obtain from Congress, then in session, the necessary appropriation.

Thus the proposed transit line to Oregon was progressing favorably when the *ultimatum* of the British Government was submitted to the President and Senate, and accepted. This at once obviated the immediate necessity for the settlement of Oregon, and as a Government matter, the proposed transit line to that part of the world was dropped. As is customary with governments on such occasions, Mr. Woodward was unceremoniously dismissed, with no thanks for the time and money he had spent in the service of the administration.

But Mr. Woodward, in the course of his efforts in behalf of the Government, had gained information respecting the commerce of the Pacific coast which induced him and several associates to believe that a line of steamers from Panama to Oregon would pay as a private enterprise, and he accordingly gave the matter this shape.

At this time Colonel Sloo was applying for a grant of subsidy to carry the mail by steam-vessels from New York to Havana and New Orleans. E. K. Collins was also endeavoring to get a bill through Congress authorizing a line of mail-steamers between New York and Liverpool.

Mr. Woodward framed his bill to cover the Pacific coast route; Sloo so changed his bill as to extend his line to Chagres, in order to connect with Woodward on the Isthmus of Darien, and all the bills, namely, Woodward's, Sloo's, and Collins', were passed on the last day of the session of 1846–'47. But either by oversight or design, Mr. Woodward's name was left out of the engrossed bill, and the Secretary of the Navy, Mr. Mason, decided that he must advertise for proposals for the Pacific line. He accordingly advertised for bids to carry the mails twice a month by steam from Panama to Astoria, in Oregon, touching at Realejo in Central America, Acapulco, Mazatlan, and Monterey in Mexico. San Francisco was not known at this time, and beyond shipping one or two cargoes of hides annually, Yerba Buena, its present site, had no commercial importance.

Mr. Woodward put in a bid of $300,000 per annum, ten years, for side-wheel steamers, and an associate bid $150,000 for propellers. One Arnold Harris, as a speculation, blundered into a bid of $199,000 per annum. These were the only bids.

The contract was awarded to Woodward's associate, who had bid $150,000 per annum for propellers, but with such conditions, not embraced in the advertisement, as made it wholly inadmissible, and the bid was withdrawn. The contract was then awarded to Harris, as the next lowest bidder. Before Woodward's associate withdrew his bid, Harris had bound himself in a bond to assign the contract to Woodward should it fall to him, Harris, by reason of such withdrawal.

The contract having fallen to Harris, he paid no regard to his bond—which proved worthless—and after receiving the contract, he hawked it about New York for several months; but as little was known respecting the proposed route, and taking into consideration the fact of the existence of the bond from Harris to Woodward, responsible parties outside of Woodward's company manifested little inclination to undertake the enterprise.

General Armstrong, then American consul at Liverpool, and a relative of Harris, now came forward and induced Mr. W. H. Aspinwall to take the matter into consideration. After a lively negotiation between the parties in New York, and the Secretary of the Navy at Washington, in which Mr. Woodward was entirely ignored, Mr. Aspinwall assumed the contract. A fierce litigation now ensued between Woodward and Harris and Aspinwall. But as usual in such cases, the brains and industry that had modestly and quietly originated and developed the enterprise to a practical point, were forced to succumb to the audacity and ravenous greed of capital, which never originates or invents.

The contract assumed by Mr. Aspinwall called for three side-wheel steamers, the first of which should sail for the Pacific in October, 1848. The California was the pioneer steamer, and she sailed for her destination at the stipulated time. The Oregon followed in November, and lastly, the Panama.

The news of the discovery of gold in California reached New York in November, 1848, about one month after the steamer California had sailed.

THE TRIP OF THE FIRST PASSENGERS FROM NEW YORK TO SAN FRANCISCO BY STEAM.

The first reports of the great discovery made but little impression on the public mind, but in a few weeks parties arrived direct from California, and their wonderful tales of auriferous developments, with the exhibition of considerable precious dust from the placers, soon gave the people the gold fever.

About the middle of December, 1848, the steamer Isthmus was advertised to sail for Chagres the 25th inst. But this steamer being delayed, the Crescent City, Captain Stoddard, was dispatched by Messrs. Howard & Sons on the 23d December, 1848. This steamer, with about one hundred and fifty passengers, myself among the number, arrived at Chagres January 2d, 1849.

Nothing of moment occurred on the voyage from New York to Chagres, except that, in a furious gale off Hatteras, a steward was washed overboard. Several large arm-chairs were thrown over to the unfortunate man as he floated past the stern of the ship, one of which he succeeded in grasping, and, thus sustained, he was finally picked up and saved by the daring and good seamanship of a Boston sea-captain commanding the life-boat, manned by four brave sailors, who, after an hour's most desperate exertion, succeeded in pulling back to the steamer, which could do nothing more than lie-to and await their return.

On reaching Chagres, we found the steamer Fulton had arrived the day before from New Orleans, with two hundred passengers. Here were nearly four hundred excited, adventurous gold-seekers congregated at this wretched place, composed of a hundred or more *jacals*, or cane huts, and inhabited by Indians, negroes, half-breeds, dogs, pigs, etc. These adventurers were robustiously frantic in their efforts to cross the isthmus and secure a passage on the steamer California, the arrival of which was daily expected at Panama. The dusky natives with their squalid children, their dogs and pigs, the monkeys, alligators, snakes, and all created things of the aligerous order, were roused from their dreamy lethargy by this sudden irruption of the Northern white race. The hubbub was terrific.

The only mode of passage across the isthmus was by boats up the Chagres River to Cruces—some thirty-five miles—and thence by pedal or quadrupedal conveyance to Panama. Every species of boat that could be poled up the river was in tremendous demand. An astonishing number of *lanchas, bungos, canoas*, etc., were speedily brought together; and in forty-eight hours from the time of their arrival, the passengers were experiencing the distressing and highly peculiar navigation of the Chagres River. Just as the larger portion had reached Cruces, the cholera, which had made its appearance on the steamer Fulton, broke out among them. The panic soon became fearful. The great body of gold-seekers rushed off for Panama, helter-skelter, pell-mell, some on mules, some on horses, and some on foot. Friend left friend to die; and men brave under other circumstances, slunk away from the danger they could not see, leaving their baggage to its fate on the river's bank, and scattered all over the town.

I had joined a party of five in arrangements to cross the isthmus together. At Cruces we occupied a cane hut, where we gathered our baggage, proposing to start for Panama after a night's stretching of our aching limbs, that had for many long hours been painfully cramped in the river boat. At four o'clock in the morning, one of our party, Mr. M——, of New York, a gentleman of most agreeable disposition, and whose acquaintance I had made on board the Crescent City, roused me, and said he felt ill. An hour later he complained of being much worse, and in low tones begged me not to desert him should his illness prove to be the cholera. I immediately found a Dr. Clements—afterward torn to pieces by a grizzly bear in California—and requested him to call and see Mr. M——. He did so, and at once pronounced him ill of cholera. In five minutes not one of my companions was visible, and in less than half an hour they were all on the road to Panama, their baggage remaining piled up in the hut. One of these was the Boston sea-captain who had so nobly risked his life in saving the steward of the Crescent City from a watery grave. That was a visible and familiar danger, against which he did not hesitate to oppose his strength, experience, and skill; but the unseen messenger of death hovering about, armed with a terrible pestilence and striking down his victims at random, was more than he could face.

Of course I assured Mr. M—— that I would remain and do all in my power to save him from the terrible malady. For fifty dollars I hired a kind-hearted Irishman—left in charge of the baggage of General Persifer F. Smith, who had passed on to Panama—to assist me; and then in the blaze and heat of the tropical sun we fought death with such slender means as under the circumstances we could command, till two o'clock, P. M., when poor M——, wasted to a perfect skeleton in a few hours, yielded up his life. He feared not death, but his distress at the thought of leaving his family was overpowering. The last words he was able to utter, some two hours before his death, were a request that if ever I got back to the city of New York, I would see his family. I complied with this request during my visit to New York, in 1853, and I could not marvel at the distress of the father as he faced death, and felt that he must part with all that was dear to him on earth forever. I met with a lovely family—the mother and six children. There was the little one just able to speak the words of gratitude as instructed by the mother, and so on, boys and girls, up to the fine youth of fifteen. As these children entered the room to meet me, they took my hand one after the other, and said, in the most touching manner, "God bless you, sir, for your kindness to our father!" This was a trying scene.

In the great revolution for good, and the happiness and comfort, direct and indirect, which we trust were among the first results of the discovery of gold in California, it must be admitted that there was also a vast amount of attendant evil, and that sorrow and misery were brought to the hearts of thousands and tens of thousands of loved and loving beings. There was scarcely a family throughout the length and breadth of the land but what was affected for good or ill during the first years of the California gold-fever.

With the assistance of several natives we buried Mr. M—— at 3 P. M., where other victims among the passengers had been laid, the Rev. Mr. Douglas performing the funeral ceremony. This clergyman remained and heroically filled his sad office till there was no longer any necessity. Mr. M—— was the last victim in Cruces. He had several trunks well filled with every thing requisite for his comfort, on the long and uncertain journey before him, all evidently prepared and packed by loving hearts and willing hands. To go through the forms required by the alcalde, and get this little property in a condition to return to the family in New York, occupied me till far into the night —and what a weary, unearthly night it was! Every passenger, except an old man, Mr. Erastus Sparrow, and Mr. Raymond, agent of the New York steamer, had departed. The natives were dying of cholera in considerable numbers; but, as usual in these Catholic countries, the poor Indians evinced a kind of stolid resignation to Fate, and resorted to religious ceremonies. During the night processions of gaunt forms, robed in long white gowns, moved through the miserable little town, chanting the *Miserere* and other doleful strains. Morning dawned at last; the black pall of night was rolled up, and the unearthly aspect of things was dispelled. I had arranged with the alcalde to take charge of my own baggage and that of my light-footed companions, and forward it by first opportunity. I now began to look about for something to carry me to Panama. But every thing with four legs that could bear a burden had been pressed into the service, and there was nothing left for me. At length I met with a very polite and scantily-clad Indian gentleman, who said that possibly he might obtain an animal for me in a few hours. Being very weary, I concluded to wait awhile, rather than start on foot. At noon the Indian brought me one of the small horses of the country, that appeared to be simply a framework of bones. I concluded, however, to take my chances with this defective beast. Before mounting to depart, I bade farewell to Mr. Sparrow, expressing the hope that we should meet at some future day in California. This desiccated old man had brought as far as Cruces a number of bales of india-rubber goods, which he declared he would stick to, cholera or no cholera; and stick to them he did. He got them over the isthmus and on board the steamer California. On arriving at San Francisco he sold his goods at enormous prices, and starting on this successful venture, the old man made a large fortune in California, where he now resides. I met him in Wall Street nearly two years ago, in great haste to complete some financial transactions, preparatory to embarking for California the next day. He casually remarked that in a few days he would be a hundred and one years old. On expressing my surprise at this, he remarked that when a boy, living in one of the back towns of Massachusetts, he heard the thunder of the cannon at the battle of Bunker Hill. Whether the old gentleman numbers between one and two hundred years or not I am unable to say. I can assert, however, that he is the oldest specimen of pluck and determination I have ever met.

There being nothing more to detain me at Cruces, I took my departure. With the exception of some of my lonely trips across the deserts of Arizona, surrounded by the merciless Apaches, I cannot remember to have been in so forlorn a situation as when I started on my solitary way from Cruces to Panama, without food for the journey, worn down by the continued excitement of painful scenes and want of rest, and with half a dozen cayenne-pepper pills in my pocket—given me by Dr. Clements—to take should I be, as others had been, attacked by cholera *en route*. To add to my troubles, the small steed furnished me by the polite and scantily-clad Indian gentleman broke down, so far as being able to carry me, before evening. I should have turned him out to grass by the roadside, but I had bound myself in writing, under the penalty of an enormous sum, compared with the value of the animal, to deliver him safe and sound to Señor Somebody in Panama; and not feeling inclined to be accessory to the swindle, I assisted the harmless creature over the rugged and steep mountain-path, and dragged him out of the mud-holes which were frequent, it being the rainy season.

In this manner, Rackabones and I slowly worked our way to within some twelve miles of Panama, when just at nightfall, as we were passing what appeared to be a deserted hut, some one within cried out, "*Halloo, stranger!*" This proved to be a fellow-passenger named F. C. Gray, who had left Cruces the evening before on foot, and now he appeared to be suffering from cholera, as he supposed, but it proved to be what became known as Panama fever. I had been in hopes of reaching an inhabited spot where something in the way of edibles could be obtained before stopping for the night. The horde of passengers had cleared Cruces and the road of every thing, and I had not tasted a mouthful since morning. Mr. Gray begged me to lodge with him, and he offered his remaining stock of provisions, a box of sardines, and some bits of hard bread. I partook of a part of these, and after making the best provision possible for my equine *protégé*, Gray and myself arranged to pass the night as comfortably as the circumstances would admit. At dawn of day, being somewhat refreshed, and Gray feeling able to proceed, we resumed our journey, driving Rackabones before us, and weighing the probabilities of the future.

This Mr. Gray reached San Francisco by the steamer California, and he was the first of the new-comers to open a gambling-saloon. Having speedily gained a large amount of money, he suddenly cut loose from the gambling fraternity, and commenced business as a banker under the firm of Graham, Gray & Co., and was elected alderman at the first charter election. This and other public offices he filled creditably until 1853, when he came to New York, purchased a fine up-town house, made every arrangement to live elegantly, and then, one fine morning, he went out to the Hudson River Railroad track, and watching his opportunity just as the train came thundering along, laid his neck on the rail and was horribly decapitated. No reason could be given for the rash act. California developed some extraordinary characters.

Three miles from Panama we came to a station, where we were able to hire mule conveyance to the city. I turned over Rackabones to the master muleteer, who promised to deliver him to the agent, and at length, in the afternoon of the 11th of January, 1849, I entered the gates of the ancient and renowned city of Panama, astride a meagre mule of cadaverous expression and remarkably long ears. My broad-brimmed Indian straw hat was in a condition to be of little use, and it certainly was not ornamental. My clothes were badly torn, and I was plastered over with mud from head to foot. Assisting that small horse—so kindly procured for me by the Indian gentleman at Cruces—across the isthmus, was the principal cause of the sorry plight in which I made my appearance at Panama. My fellow-passengers had given me up as a victim to the cholera, and now they could only recognize me as a spirit from the vasty deep—of mud.

The passengers were now congregated at Panama, awaiting the steamer California *via* Cape Horn, fully due. The steamer might arrive at any hour, or, if an accident had befallen her, she might not arrive for weeks. The absorbing interest of this point, with the better accommodations afforded in Panama, had caused the cholera panic to abate, though cases of both cholera and Panama fever were constantly occurring in the city; but in a short time the cholera disappeared entirely. Considering the bad season, the fatigue and exposure in crossing the isthmus, the lack of accommodations and medical attendance, with the imprudent indulgences of many of the strangers, it is remarkable that a larger number were not swept off by the fell destroyer.

I had secured my passage on the steamer California before leaving New York. Others had done the same; but the majority were obliged to take the chance of obtaining a passage at Panama. The anxious state of mind that prevailed among the latter can well be imagined.

Having secured comfortable quarters, and rested a day or two, I joined a party of four in a whaleboat excursion down the bay—fifteen miles—to the Island of Taboga, now the station of the Pacific Mail Steamship Company.

Like a mass of molten gold, the waters of the bay, in sluggish swells and coquettish ripples, darted back the solar rays. It all looked very pleasant and very inviting, and there appeared to be nothing but tropical heat to mar the pleasures of the excursion, and a row to the island lying in the calm, golden haze of the horizon seemed to be an easy matter. But it proved otherwise, as it required hard pulling nearly all day to reach our landing. We were well rewarded, however, for our exertions. Modern utilitarianism had not broken in upon the primitive loveliness of this tropical island gem, nor obliterated the paradisiacal aspect that in gentleness and peace had rested there upon things animate and inanimate from the time Eve tempted and Adam fell; and which, in a few years, cannot, in view of commercial progress, be found in any spot on earth.

The beach was strewn with singing shells of exquisite tints and beautifully mottled; balmy breezes tempered the tropical heat, and delicious waters leaped in silvery cascades over rocks on the hill-sides, and murmured through the dells. The pine-apple, orange, banana, and other rich fruits, were seen amid groves of the tamarind, cocoanut, mango, and palm; vines ran in festoons from tree to tree, and hung in swaying pendants from the branches; flowers of brilliant hue enlivened the landscape, while birds of gaudy plumage fluttered and sang in bush and tree; and lovely Indian maidens, who dreamed away life in a voluptuous atmosphere that invited to blissful relaxation and repose, bathed in rock-bound pools of cool, crystal waters, found in picturesque recesses hidden by a network of foliage and flowers.

So charming did the island appear, that we determined, on receiving our baggage at Panama, to return and await the arrival of the steamer California, in this lovely and healthy spot. Having secured a commodious Indian hut, we started for Panama early the next morning. Before a third of the distance had been made, signs of a heavy blow appeared, and soon a furious gale struck us on our starboard bow. There was but one practical sailor on board —the Boston sea-captain—and now in our perilous situation he did us good service. We could not make headway against the winds and waves; we could only drift toward the mainland, lying some distance to the northwest. The boat was driven into an estuary of the bay, toward a coast that appeared precipitous and rocky, with here and there a patch of sand-beach, which by the rolling of the breakers appeared to be somewhat shelving. We knew we were to be dashed upon this coast, and that every thing depended upon our being able to so guide the boat that the breakers would throw it upon one of the patches of sand-beach instead of dashing it against the rocks, where our destruction would be inevitable. A few rods to the right or to the left, and we would be hurled against the rocks and lost. On we were driven, riding the crest of the furious waves as nothing but a whaleboat can ride, direct for the little haven that promised a chance for life, until seized upon by the last breaker. Here we lost all control of the boat, and at one moment we appeared to be making directly for the rocks, and at the next we were whirled past within a few feet and cast high and dry on the patch of sand-beach for which we had steered, but with a shock that partially stove the upper works on one side of the boat, and threw us out with stunning violence. All were more or less bruised, and one of the party received an injury in the spine from which he never recovered.

It was now late in the afternoon, our water and provisions all consumed, the raging sea on one side, a high, steep bank crested with chaparral on the other, and one of the party disabled. Placing our boat beyond the reach of the angry waves, we at once commenced scrambling up the bank and working our way inland through the chaparral in search of something human. The country appeared wild and desolate, and should it prove to be entirely uninhabited, our situation would be in the highest degree deplorable. For an hour we continued our painful exploration, tearing our clothes and flesh in the dense chaparral, and encountering nothing but all sorts of snakes, lizards, and detestable bugs and flies. At length we struck a trail, which, in a few moments, led us to an open patch of ground and an Indian hut, where our eyes were gladdened by the sight of *ollas* of cool water and plenty of chickens and yams. The Indians were kind and hospitable. They cooked for us; we ate and drank, and soon our bodily pains were forgotten in " Nature's sweet restorer, balmy sleep."

The first question in the morning was, how

to get back to Panama, sixty miles distant by land, and only reached by circuitous and blind Indian paths. By sea the distance was twenty miles, more than a day's hard pull, according to our experience, saying nothing of the uncertainty of the winds and waves. Ingenuity solved the difficulty. Noticing the light but tightly-woven and strong mats used by the natives to lie or sit upon, we purchased two of our kind Indian host, and by sewing them together with *pita*, we made a very respectable spritsail; with nothing but a *machete* we worked out a mast, and, well supplied with strips of hide for strings and ropes, we repaired to the shore, not more than half a mile distant, guided by the Indian through a well-beaten path. We stepped the mast and rigged the sail; the gale had subsided, but the sea still rolled heavily, and, as the best part of the day was spent, we concluded to return to the Indian's hut for the night, and take an early start in the morning. At dawn of day, being well supplied with water, boiled chicken, and yams, we again repaired to the shore, to find a smooth sea and a dead calm. Fate appeared to be against us. We waited till

11 o'clock, when the sea-breeze sprang up. At 12 M., the tide served, we launched our boat, spread our sail, and put out. The novel sail worked so well that we were able to dispense with the white-ash breeze, except for the last mile or two, and just as the shades of evening fell we landed at the mole in Panama, with a wholesome experience that taught us the hardship and uncertainty attending rowing excursions in those waters.

The next morning, all the baggage I left in charge of the alcalde at Cruces arrived, and I arranged to return to the Island of Taboga the following day. But I was suddenly taken with the cholera, and in view of the fatigue and hardships to which I had been exposed, I promised to be a ready victim. The cholera was subsiding in Panama, and having escaped thus far, I had ceased to consider myself in any great danger of being attacked by this dreadful malady. But it struck me at last, and for a short time the conflict between life and death was terrible. In the midst of this desperate struggle I had consciousness enough left to be aware that something extraordinary was taking place in the city. My lodgings were near the sea-wall and facing the bay. Suddenly there was a rush of people and the trampling of many feet directly under my window. There were discordant shouts and cries, and then the shout went up in and around the house, "*Steamer coming! steamer coming!*" A dark speck had been discerned in the horizon, seaward, then a murky streak, and finally the black hull of a steamer appeared coming rapidly up the bay. It proved to be the long and anxiously expected steamer California. This was the 17th day of January, 1849.

The effect on myself was magical. The power of will revived with tenfold vigor, and this, with the kind and assiduous care of Dr. Samuel Haley, soon gained the victory. Life conquered, death vanished, and in a few days I was able to sit up, and from my window look out upon the first American steamer that ever floated in Pacific waters, riding proudly at anchor in the harbor of Panama.

With the arrival of the steamer California at Panama commenced scenes of wild excitement, which continued for days and even weeks.

Here were congregated hundreds of adventurers, many of them wild and reckless, and all more or less actuated by the most powerful motives by which man is moved, namely, fear, or a desire to flee from a sickly place on the one hand, and the *auri sacra fames* on the other; and but few of all these had their passage secured on the steamer California.

It will be remembered that no news of the discovery of gold in California had reached New York when the steamer California sailed for the Pacific, and she had been fitted up to accommodate only about seventy-five passengers. No sooner, therefore, had she dropped anchor in the harbor of Panama, than Zachary & Nelson, the agents of the steamer, directed that every arrangement to carry the largest number of passengers possible should be made. The fitting up and placing on board the necessary supplies would require ten or twelve days. During this period the contest to obtain passage tickets on the steamer raged, and the excitement was increased by the arrival of passengers brought to Cruces by sailing vessels and steamers. It was finally discovered that no tickets could be sold by the agents in Panama, as the office in New York had actually over-sold the passenger capacity of the steamer. What added fuel to the flame, was the fact that the steamer on touching at Callao, on her way up the Pacific coast, had received on board some seventy-five Peruvians as steerage passengers, the news of the discovery of gold in California having reached that region. "What right," exclaimed the ticketless passengers, "has an American steamer to give passage to wretched *greasers*, when so many honest American miners are awaiting a conveyance to American territory to dig American gold?"

Indignation meetings were held in front of the office of Zachary & Nelson, of the hotels, and on the plaza. It is doubtful whether the ancient city of Panama, in the old buccaneer times, ever witnessed such continued scenes of uproar, excitement, and confusion, as reigned throughout the place during the sojourn of the first California gold-seekers.

But the steamer was declared ready at last, and all who had tickets were taken on board. The passengers numbered over five hundred, and there were as many more remaining at Panama, to find their way to California by sailing vessels, or by the steamer Oregon, the next of the California line—due in February. I had sufficiently recovered to go on board with a number of other cholera and Panama-fever convalescents. Among the passengers were General Persifer F. Smith and staff; John McDougall, the first Governor of the State after it was admitted into the Union; Hardin Bigelow, first mayor of Sacramento City; Rodman M. Price, then purser in the Navy, since Governor of New Jersey; T. B. Van Buren, Esq., now Colonel Van Buren, of New York; the Rev. Messrs. Wheeler, Wiley, and Douglass, with others who became more or less distinguished.

The California steamed out of Panama Bay on the last day of January, 1849. The after-cabin was crowded, and every part of the forward-cabin—in reality the steerage—was fitted up with bunks, while the poor Peruvians were permitted to make themselves as comfortable as circumstances would admit, on the upper deck. This ship, of eleven hundred tons, was literally alive with human beings.

We had not been at sea forty-eight hours, before serious trouble arose among the steerage or forward-cabin passengers, respecting the food with which they were furnished, the horrible stench and filth that prevailed, and the utter neglect of the agents and officers to provide for the comfort of those who from necessity had taken passage in that part of the ship. It was evident to all that positive suffering throughout the passage would be the consequence.

Morning, noon, and night, those passengers were fed like so many animals on wormy *charqui* or jerked beef, old and musty hard bread, and miserable coffee. These passengers were not, for the most part, of the class usually found in the steerage. There were lawyers, doctors, merchants, and clergymen, with many others, who went in the steerage because by no possible means could they go in the cabin. There were also those who turned out to be thieves, robbers, blacklegs, and murderers. The educated and the ignorant, the refined and the vulgar, the good and the bad, saints and sinners, were huddled together in the hold of that ship without distinction. All had paid a high price for their passage; several had purchased their tickets second-hand, and given a thousand dollars bonus. They did not expect cabin fare, but they demanded palatable food as their right, and when they found this could not be obtained, their indignation knew no bounds.

The first move of the sufferers was to appoint a committee—not an unusual proceeding with an American constituency—to wait on the captain, and represent their grievances. The eloquence of the chairman of the committee, a first-class butcher, was more forcibly direct than persuasively elegant. "Is that crawling stuff," said he, pointing to a kid of beef that had been placed before the captain, "the kind of food to crowd down the throats of free-born Americans?" With all the serious points in the matter, this scene was ludicrous in the extreme.

Captain Cleveland Forbes brought the ship from New York to Panama, and although he remained on board—being much out of health —the ship was in charge of one Captain Marshall, an excellent navigator, a well-meaning man, and apparently desirous of doing all in his power to make the passengers comfortable. But Captain Marshall lacked force of will, and decision, and at the very start he lost all control of the passengers, especially those in the steerage, who numbered four-fifths of all on board. These passengers virtually had possession of the ship from the beginning to the end of the voyage. They simply permitted the engineer to manage the engine, and the captain to do the navigation.

To the committee on food, Captain Marshall respectfully replied, that the ship sailed from Panama under an emergency. There was a great crowd of passengers clamoring to get on board to go to California. Nothing of the kind had been anticipated when the ship left New York, and they had not been able to fully prepare for this unexpected state of things. The best provisions that Panama afforded had been purchased for the voyage, and if they proved of bad quality it was not his fault.

The passengers acknowledged the truth of all this, except the statement that the best provisions Panama afforded had been purchased.

On this and minor points the excitement continued, and soon there were scenes of violence around the cook's quarters. A band of roughs, their anger excited, and their appetites whetted by the sight and smell of savory dishes cooked for the cabin, attacked the cook and stewards, drove them from the cook-house, and took forcible possession of the viands. These scenes of violence occurred on several consecutive days, greatly to the discomfort of the cabin passengers; and there were signs of further serious mischief brewing, when we entered the harbor of Acapulco.

This brought temporary relief. All the passengers who could afford it, laid in such supplies as could be obtained—eggs, fresh bread, fresh and dried fruits, good coffee, etc., etc., and after the ship had taken in a supply of water, we again put to sea.

In a few days the fresh provisions were all consumed, and general demoralization again prevailed. The blasphemy in the steerage became terrific—a phenomenon. One of the most distinguished clergymen now residing in San Francisco was in the steerage. His nature was as sensitive and gentle as that of a woman. The roughest of the passengers treated him with the greatest kindness, and when on Sunday he performed divine service, their violence and terrible blasphemy subsided, and meek as lambs they listened to the words of the man of God.

I asked this clergyman what he thought of such blasphemy, and I was struck with the discretion and sound philosophy evinced by his reply. He said it was certainly hard swearing, but the circumstances under which it occurred were exceptional. Such a human cargo, so much savage energy and active enterprise, were never before pent up in one small ship under such peculiar circumstances. There was much to irritate, and every thing to excite to an extraordinary degree; and while the passengers were angry on some points relating to the ship, they felt truly kind toward each other, and on the whole the swearing did not amount to much. A harsher view of the matter, and denunciation, would only make matters worse.

We were now making for the port of Mazatlan, and when within a day's sail of the place, the wheels of the steamer began to turn slowly, and gradually they ceased moving altogether. For a time the cause of this stoppage was not made known, but finally it was announced that the firemen had mutinied and refused to perform their duty any longer. These firemen were actually sustained in their mutinous proceedings by the rougher portion of the steerage passengers; and such was the general demoralization of the ship, and so completely had the officers lost all control, that for several hours we lay rolling about like a log in a pretty rough sea, and no attempt made to fire up and move on our course. But the perversity of human nature being satisfied at last, the firemen again went to work, and in due time we anchored in the harbor of Mazatlan. The captain here showed pluck and determination for the first time. With the aid of the Mexican authorities he seized the ringleaders of the mutinous firemen, put them on shore, and shipped Mexicans in their place. Again the passengers refreshed themselves with the good things of Mazatlan, and obtained temporary relief on board ship by taking in a supply of such provisions as the place afforded, without which they could not have been sustained to the end of the voyage. A few days out from Mazatlan, the same state of demoralization prevailed, and the scenes of riot and confusion were of frequent occurrence. All this arose from the fact that at the several ports made by the steamer, the officers, with singular fatuity, while doing nothing to ameliorate the condition of the steerage passengers, took in, right before their eyes, fresh supplies for the cabin.

Thus matters stood until within three hundred miles of Monterey, in California, when the steamer's wheels again came to a dead stand. None of the passengers could imagine the cause, but soon it was announced that every pound of coal had been consumed! This, indeed, was a serious matter, something calculated to restore order, and sober everybody. Three hundred miles from port, five hundred half-starved passengers, a short supply of water and provisions, and few vessels then to be met with in that part of the world; no steam, no sails rigged, and heavy gales of frequent occurrence at that season; not the most agreeable prospect, it must be acknowledged.

But something must be done. The ship was heeled over, to throw one of the wheels out of water, and men were set at work to take off the floats. The sails that had been stored in New York were got out, and such as could be were bent. But so tightly were the floats held in the rusty iron bands, that after working nearly a whole day, but one float was removed. This proceeding was then abandoned, the ship righted, and all sail possible was spread, in the hope that fair headway might be made. But even with a fair wind the ship did not move a knot an hour, and it was evident that some other mode of getting out of the difficulty must be devised. Hour by hour matters grew worse, and the prospect became more gloomy. Something must be done. A consultation was held on the quarter-deck, and it was resolved to burn every spar and plank, every piece of wood that could be cut or torn from the inside of the ship without endangering the hull, in the hope that steam might be kept up until we could reach Monterey.

Tackles were at once rigged, and the work of raising spare plank, spars, etc., from the lower hold commenced. Every axe and saw on board was put in requisition, and the passengers went to work with a will, although some of those in the steerage appeared to take a sullen delight in the difficulty, and it actually seemed as though they would willingly go to the bottom of the sea could they but take the ship with them and spite the owners.

The work of gathering planks, spars, etc., and of sawing, cutting, splitting, and smashing went on vigorously all over the ship. Steam was raised, and the ship turned on her course. But the last planks and spars were being raised from the hold, the demolition of berths in both steerage and cabin had already commenced, when it became evident that all the wood that could be got out of the inside of the ship would not keep up steam but a few hours, and a heavy gloom was beginning to settle down upon the passengers, when all were electrified by the cry of "*Coal! coal! coal!*" On taking up the last planks and spars in the lower hold, there were discovered lying on the keel a hundred bags of coal, shipped in New York as ballast, and the fact was not known to any officer or other individual on board.

The work of cutting and sawing wood ceased, the coal was raised, and we continued on our way rejoicing. But now another difficulty was encountered. As we neared the coast a dense fog prevailed, and for nearly a whole day we groped about where we supposed the entrance to Monterey Bay should be.

Our newly-found supply of coal was being rapidly consumed, and matters again began to look somewhat dubious, when the fog lifted for a few moments, and Purser Price, who had been on that coast before, got hold of what he was very certain were the headlands at the entrance of Monterey Bay; and taking the course indicated by Mr. Price, we steered through the dense fog directly into Monterey harbor, and the fires were getting low, for want of coal, when we came to anchor.

We remained in Monterey a week to obtain a supply of wood sufficient to carry us to San Francisco, ninety miles distant. Captain Marshall offered five dollars per day to every passenger who would chop wood. Numbers in the condition known as "strapped" accepted the offer, and having got on board an adequate supply of the fuel, we put to sea for the last time. After a rapid run we entered the Golden Gate, and amid the thunder of cannon, the shouts of the people of San Francisco, and their wild rejoicings, we anchored in the bay on the 28th day of February, 1849, sixty-seven days from New York, and twenty-nine days from Panama.

Thus ended the eventful trip of the first passengers from New York to California, and thus terminated the extraordinary voyage of the first steamer from Panama to San Francisco, having come round Cape Horn, the pioneer of the Pacific Mail Steamship Company's line. It is somewhat of a marvel that the steamer arrived in San Francisco with all her passengers safe and sound. But not a single death occurred, and no sickness worth mentioning. There was too much excitement, too much indignation on board to allow of any sickness. The ship was on fire several times, but these fires were extinguished without any general or serious alarm. Considerable heavy weather was encountered, but nothing that caused damage to the ship. The short supply of coal, the bad food, the filth, and the demoralized and mutinous state of feeling that prevailed in consequence, were the sources of the principal trouble, and these came very near being productive of serious disaster.

Seventeen years have passed since the occurrence of the events just narrated. Captains Cleveland and Marshall, General Persifer F. Smith, Governor McDougall, and Mayor Bigelow, are all dead. At a meeting of surviving passengers held a year ago in San Francisco, to celebrate the anniversary of the arrival of the steamer California, February 28, 1849, I understand that nineteen only of the five hundred passengers who then landed, could be counted as still being in the land of the living. There are, no doubt, many more in existence, scattered throughout different parts of the world, and they doubtless retain a vivid recollection of the excitement of the time, and the extraordinary scenes through which they passed.

It will be perceived that the Pacific mail-steamers were built and dispatched just in season to accommodate the first rush of passengers to California. It had required nearly three years to originate the line, obtain the contract from the Government, build the steamers, and dispatch them to the Pacific. Astoria was to have been the northern terminus of the line; San Francisco was not mentioned. This enterprise, in connection with Sloo's line to New Orleans and Chagres, could not have been timed more opportunely to meet the necessities of the case.

I have now described that remarkable combination of events antecedent to the discovery of gold in California, adding thereto, as an interesting incident of the time, and a personal reminiscence, an account of the trip of the first passengers from New York to San Francisco.

We see that the English were just too late; the Bear flag was just behind time, so were the Mormons. The American flag was raised in California exactly in the nick of time, and the war with Mexico ended just as opportunely. The gold was discovered at Sutter's Mill not a moment too soon or too late; the United States closed the bargain for California on the very day the gold was discovered, and the Pacific Mail and Sloo's lines of steamers were ready at the precise moment they were wanted to accommodate the immense treasure, mail, and passenger business that immediately sprang up between the old States and the Pacific shores. All these events culminated between July, 1846, and February, 1848, a period of only eighteen months.

NO POSITIVE KNOWLEDGE OF THE EXISTENCE OF GOLD IN CALIFORNIA, PREVIOUS TO ITS DISCOVERY.

It should be borne in mind that any discovery of gold in California, or positive knowledge of its existence, or any well-grounded belief that this precious metal would be found in considerable quantities in that territory, formed, up to this time, little or no part of the attractions of the country, and had no influence in causing the remarkable combination of events just described.

Every section of country in the New World was, at the time of its discovery, reported as being rich in the precious metals. Voyagers and explorers made the most extravagant and reckless statements respecting the quantity of gold and silver to be found in the lands they visited. California is thus mentioned in the history of the early voyagers.

Hakluyt, in his account of the first voyage of discovery made by Sir Francis Drake to the coast of California in 1577, says: "There is no part of the earth here to be taken up wherein there is not some special likelihood of gold and silver."

Another account says: "The earth of the country seemed to promise rich veins of gold and silver, some of the ore being constantly found on digging."

Pinkerton, in his description of Drake's voyage, remarks: "The land is so rich in gold and silver, that upon the slightest turning it up with a spade or pick-axe, these rich metals plainly appear mixed with the mould."

A priest of the mission of San José, bay of San Francisco, named Loyala Cavello, on returning to Spain, published, in 1690, a work on Upper California, in which he stated the occurrence of gold in placers.

The Historico-Geographical Dictionary of Antonio de Alcedo, 1786–'89, positively asserts the existence of gold in California, even in lumps of five to eight pounds.

Humboldt visited Mexico in 1803. He went as far north as Mazatlan, and after exploring the mining districts of the interior, worked by the Spaniards, he made the remarkable statement—as will be found in the narrative of his travels—that in his opinion the precious metals, which in that portion of Mexico were only reached at great depth, would be found in large quantities near the surface in the extreme northern part of the Spanish possessions, referring to what are now the Territories of Arizona and New Mexico, and, the States of Nevada, Colorado, and California.

The Penny Cyclopædia of 1836 thus disposes of the matter: "In minerals Upper California is not rich. A small silver mine has been found east of St. Ines, but it has been abandoned. In one of the rivers falling into the southern Tulare lakes, gold has been found, but as yet in very small quantities."

In 1837, a priest went from California to Guatemala, and by his representations induced Mr. Young Anderson, a Scotch gentleman, to attempt to enlist English capital for the purpose of exploring for gold *in the vicinity of San Francisco.* The scheme was regarded in England as quixotic.

Prof. J. J. Dana, of Wilkes's exploring expedition, came across the land from Oregon to Sutter's Fort in 1842, and, in his geological report of the country, he mentioned the favorable appearance of both California and Oregon for gold.

One Dr. Sanders, a Swede of scientific attainments, and who had resided in Mexico, was sent by the Duke of Bedford to explore California. He explored the Butte Mountains, and all that region, in 1843, and on leaving the country he told Captain Sutter that he found evidences of gold in the mountains, but he would not advise him to search for it, as, in his opinion, it would only pay a government to work the mines, should any be found. "Your mine," said Dr. Sanders, "is in the soil."

On the 21st of December, 1846, L. W. Sloat, Esq., who had made a brief visit to California, read a very interesting paper before the Lyceum of Natural History, in New York, in which he expressed his views relative to the existence of gold, silver, etc., throughout that territory, in the following positive manner: "There is not the least doubt in my mind, from all the information I was enabled to obtain during my stay in California, that gold, silver, quicksilver, copper, lead, sulphur, asphaltum, and coal, are to be found in all that region; and I am confident that when it becomes settled—as it soon will be by Americans—the mineral developments will greatly exceed in richness and rarity the most sanguine expectations."

Now to the careless reader all this would be considered a strong record, and it would seem as though the existence of gold in California, in quantities as discovered in our day, has been known from the time of Drake's first voyage in 1577. But a little intelligent investigation of the subject will show that all these extravagant representations respecting the existence of the precious metals in California were utterly baseless.

The statements of the existence of an abundance of gold and silver, such as those of Hakluyt, Pinkerton, Cavello, and Alcedo, must have been purely imaginary. Those of Drake's his-

THE DISCOVERY OF GOLD IN CALIFORNIA. 97

torians especially are perfectly absurd. Neither gold nor silver has as yet been found in any part of California that Drake and his companions ever saw or heard of.

Gold is not found on the coast, in the Coast Range of mountains, nor in the valleys beyond. It is not found until the spurs of the Sierra Nevada range, two or three hundred miles from the coast, are reached; and the silver district is located still further in the interior. Both gold and silver were found at last in an entirely different region of the territory from that in which their existence was predicted.

Another evidence of defects in the histories of voyages and explorations in those days is the fact that when California was first discovered and occupied by the Europeans, not an ounce of gold or silver was found among the aborigines! and they were possessed of no description of metal. Their rude implements of peace and war were made of wood, stone, or bone. The only ornaments discovered among them were chains of bone and crowns of network, wrought with feathers of many colors.

Captain Woode Rogers, who touched on the coast of Lower California in 1709, describes the aborigines as quite naked, except that the women wore a short petticoat, reaching scarcely to the knees, and made of grass, or the skins of pelicans or deer. Some of them wore pearls around their necks, which they fastened with a string of silk-grass, having first notched them all round; and Captain Rogers imagined they did not know how to bore them. These pearls were mixed with sticks, bits of shells, and little red berries.

It is a singular fact that during the several ages California was claimed and occupied by the Spaniards, and down to the period when gold was actually discovered at Sutter's Mill, not a single event of special moment had occurred tending to excite attention on the subject of the existence of an abundance of gold in that territory, or cause any effort to be made for its discovery.

It is true that in 1842 a gold placer was found in the vicinity of San Fernando, twenty miles east of Los Angeles. About $14,000 were taken out of this placer in the course of a year by the inhabitants, and sold to the Boston traders. This discovery created no particular excitement. The placer was supposed to have been worked out, and nothing more was thought of it. It is possible that the existence of other small placers may have been known. But placer gold diggings were not, at this time, considered of much importance in any portion of Spanish America. The inhabitants simply scratched over the surface, and washed or blew out the dirt in small wooden troughs or bowls called *bateas*. They knew nothing of bed-rock, or the natural tendency of loose gold to deposit itself thereon.

It is true that common report says the Jesuit fathers who established the missions on the coast knew of the existence of gold in California in large quantities, and that they concealed their knowledge. I made this a subject of special inquiry when in California, but nothing was elicited to sustain such a report. On the contrary, old native Californians told me that they never heard or believed any thing of the kind. No missions were ever established in those regions where the gold was found at last, or in the interior valleys in California. They had no *tradition* in California, even among the Indians, respecting the existence there of the precious metals. General Sutter informed me that he had often asked the Indians to search for specimens of minerals. They would bring him blue, red, and white clay and colored stones, but never any thing indicating the presence of gold or other metals.

Hundreds of thousands of eager gold-seekers have overrun California, and prospected every nook and corner of the State. In working the mines, mountains have been tunnelled, hills torn down, valleys shafted, and rivers taken from their beds and carried long distances through other channels. The immense masses of earth displaced all over the mining regions afford an example of the tremendous energies of man thirsting for gold never equalled. Yet all this penetration of the earth and overthrow of its surface have failed to elicit a particle of evidence going to prove a preëxisting knowledge of the fact that gold lay hidden in soil and rock, or that any thing in the shape of humanity above or different from the miserable Digger Indians now found there, ever inhabited the country. Neither on the coast is there any evidence that the country was ever peopled by a different race of beings than such as were in occupation when we went there.

California, with her fine climate, magnificent mountains, lovely hills and valleys, and boundless wealth—California, so blessed by Nature, so well adapted to the development of the highest degree of perfection, mental and physical, attainable by man, and destined to be the home of an advanced civilization, has remained from time immemorial a virgin land. In no country in the world has there been so little found to interest the antiquarian. During the unknown past this Queen of the Pacific has concealed her charms and her riches, to bestow them on the daring, energetic adventurers from over the mountains.

The people of no state ever indulged in more extravagant predictions of its future greatness than did the Californians—especially those residing in San Francisco, for several years previous to the discovery of the gold-mines, as the columns of the *Alta California*, the diminutive journal of that day, will abundantly testify. But these extravagant predictions were not based, in any particular degree, on the supposed existence of any great quantity of the precious metals in the Territory. Other interests were the more prominent, and when the gold was discovered, the Californians were as much astonished as anybody else; and on the first breaking out of the gold-fever in the Territory, San Francisco having been nearly depopulated thereby, one conservative and unbelieving citizen of the place expressed his views in the following communication to the *Alta California* of May 24, 1848:

"I doubt, sir, if ever the sun shone upon such a farce as is now being enacted in California, though I fear it may prove a tragedy before the curtain drops. I consider it your duty, Mr. Editor, as a conservator of the public morals and welfare, to raise your voice against the thing. It is to be hoped that General Mason will dispatch the volunteers to the scene of action, and send these unfortunate people to their homes, and prevent others from going thither."

From the foregoing historical facts, it appears that neither in positive discovery, indication, or tradition, was there sufficient to establish the fact that gold would be found in California in paying quantities. The fine harbor of San Francisco, so admirably located to command the commerce of the North Pacific coast, and to open a trade of unlimited extent with the islands of the Pacific, and with the Asiatic shores; the extensive agricultural districts of the Territory, and its immense capacity for stock-raising, fine climate, and the *vague idea* that some day large quantities of minerals might be found, constituted the chief attractions appertaining to Upper California when it came into the possession of the United States.

SUTTER'S CONDITION IN 1848.

Resuming the direct narrative of the discovery of gold at Sutter's Mill, early in 1848, we find that Captain Sutter was then the undisputed possessor of almost boundless tracts of land, including the former Russian possessions of Ross and Bodega, and the site of the present city of Sacramento. He had performed all the conditions of his land-grants, built his fort, and completed many costly improvements. At an expense of $25,000, he had cut a mill-race three miles long, and nearly finished a new flouring-mill. He had expended $10,000 in the erection of a saw-mill near Coloma; one thousand acres of virgin soil were laid down to wheat, promising a yield of forty thousand bushels; and extensive preparations had been made for other crops. He owned eight thousand cattle, two thousand horses and mules, two thousand sheep, and one thousand swine.

Captain Sutter raised the American flag on his fort July 11, 1846. Subsequently Lieutenant Missroon, of the United States Navy, came up and organized a garrison for the fort, mostly of Sutter's own men—whites and Indians—and gave Sutter the command, which he held until peace was declared. He was also appointed alcalde of the district by Commodore Stockton, and Indian agent by General Kearney.

Such was Captain Sutter's situation when the gold was discovered on his premises. Truly, he could say:

"I am monarch of all I survey,
My right there is none to dispute."

And here our pioneer lived like a baron of old, with his people, and his flocks and herds around him, untramelled by the conventionalities of artificial society, and undisturbed by the din and turmoil of compact civilization.

Sutter's sympathies were with the United States, and his affiliations were with the citizens of the great Republic. In all his acts he manifested that love of liberty and of the republican form of government which characterizes his countrymen in so eminent a degree; and all of Sutter's aspirations and efforts were to the end that, in some legitimate manner, California should be brought into the American Union.

MARSHALL.

But there is another pioneer, humble in origin and pretensions, yet holding a prominent position in the discovery of gold in California. This is JAMES W. MARSHALL, who emigrated from New Jersey to Oregon in 1843, and from Oregon to California in 1844. Here he engaged in farming and stock-raising in a small way until the breaking out of the Mexican War, when he enlisted in the California battalion under Fremont, served faithfully throughout his term of enlistment, and received an honorable discharge. Returning home, Marshall found his horses and cattle gone—some strayed and others stolen—and in order to obtain means to buy other stock and put his place to rights, he applied to Captain Sutter for work. Marshall was then about thirty-eight years of age, unmarried, faithful, eccentric, and exceedingly stubborn. He obtained immediate employment from Captain Sutter, and proved an ingenious mechanic; making himself quite useful in the construction of chairs, tables, and all those articles of household furniture so much needed in a new settlement.

LOCATION OF THE SAW-MILL.

Lumber was in great demand among the settlers of the Sacramento valley, their numbers having been considerably augmented by the arrival of Mormons and others from over the mountains. Marshall being a good judge of the article, and otherwise competent to manage the enterprise, he was dispatched by Captain Sutter, with an Indian guide and interpreter, May, 1847, to the mountains to select the site for a saw-mill. Marshall returned and reported that he had found a good location on the south fork of the American River, forty miles east of the Fort, and at a point called by the Indians Cul-loo-ma, now called Coloma. The water-power was good, pine trees were plenty, and a Mexican cart could pass without difficulty between the fort and the proposed site of the saw-mill. Some delay occurred, and it was not until August, 1847, that Captain Sutter finally arranged with Marshall to superintend the erection and running of the saw-mill.

DISCOVERY OF THE GOLD.

The saw-mill was completed in January, 1848, and they had just commenced sawing lumber when, on the night of February 2, 1848, Marshall appeared at Sutter's Fort, his horse in a foam and himself presenting a singular appearance—all bespattered with mud, and laboring under an extraordinary degree of excitement. He immediately requested Captain Sutter to go with him into a room where they could be alone. This request was granted, and after the door was closed, Marshall asked Captain Sutter if he was sure they would not be disturbed, and desired that the door might be locked. Captain Sutter did not know what to make of his actions, and he began to think it hazardous to lock himself in the room with Marshall, who appeared so uncommonly strange.

Marshall being satisfied at last that they would not be interrupted, took from his pocket a pouch from which he poured upon the table about an ounce of yellow grains of metal which he thought would prove to be gold. Captain Sutter inquired where he got it. Marshall stated that in the morning, the water being shut off from the saw-mill race, as was customary, he discovered, in passing through the race, shining particles here and there on the bottom. On examination he found them to be of metallic substance, and the thought flashed over him that they might be gold. *How big with events was this point of time!*

SUTTER'S SAW-MILL, COLOMA.

Marshall stated that the laborers—white and Indian—had picked up some of the particles, and he thought a large quantity could be collected.

Captain Sutter was at first quite incredulous as to these particles being gold, but happening to have a bottle of nitric acid among his stores, he applied the test, and, true enough, the yellow grains proved to be pure gold. *The great discovery was made!*

View these men as they sit at the hour of midnight in the dimly lighted room of that adobe fort, located far up the Sacramento, the other side of the world to everybody but themselves, isolated, all unknowing and unknown; one an educated, polished gentleman from Europe, the other a plain, honest mechanic from the United States. Regard them as they examine those little yellow grains and learn that they are gold. The action of no king on his throne, no warrior at the head of his army, no statesman or legislative body that ever existed, was more conducive to events of the highest import to the human race, than was that of these two humble, private individuals, when they sat at the midnight hour, secluded and lonely, in that remote conntry, and discovered that they were handling gold.

What a subject for the dramatist! What a scene for the painter! This was the *dénouement* of the plot in the drama Omnipotence was enacting in California.

It must not be forgotten that another scene in this omnipotent drama was being enacted in the Mexican capital. On the very day, perhaps the very moment that Marshall discovered the grains of gold in Sutter's mill-race, the treaty that closed the Mexican War and gave us California, was signed in the city of Mexico!

The acquisition of California, and the discovery of gold, are events beyond the range of man's calculation in their influence on the destiny of the great American Republic. Though the occurrence of those two events on the same day is a startling coincidence, there is no mystery about it—nothing that need arouse the nonsense of superstition. Age by age we can clearly trace the footsteps of time coming down, period by period, with unerring precision, to those occurrences that have precipitated the

United States onward in their course of empire with a bewildering rapidity. Columbus had discovered America, and the Spaniard had enforced his bloody, soul-crushing Christianity from ocean to ocean, and from Terra del Fuego to the everglades of Florida, where Ponce de Leon searched for the waters of youth. A little more than two centuries after the landing of the Spaniard, the Anglo-Saxons appeared on the Atlantic shores of the northern portion of the continent, and one by one the colonies and peculiar institutions of the race were planted from Nova Scotia to the Mexican Gulf. Then the American Revolution gave birth to a new nation, which created a republic that soon acquired the Louisiana territory and Florida, and extended to the Pacific shore. The native races had thrown off the Spanish yoke, and republics skirted the Andes and Cordilleras, from Chili to California. Stephen Austin, of Connecticut, had obtained the consent of Mexico to colonize the Province of Texas with North Americans; and these, bringing their slaves into the province, contrary to Mexican law, caused the beginning of trouble with Mexico, which resulted in the war that gave Texas her independence, which led to annexation to the United States. This brought on the war with Mexico, which resulted in peace and the acquisition of New Mexico and California, February 2, 1848.

Now look at another class of events, tending directly to the same great end. Sutter, born in 1803, the year in which we acquired the Louisiana territory, had emigrated from Europe and settled in the Missouri portion of that territory. From thence, after five years' wandering in New Mexico, over the Rocky Mountains, through Oregon, to the Sandwich Islands, and the Russian possessions, he had located in the wild and isolated Sacramento valley, built his fort, subdued the country, established an extensive and flourishing colony; and all this occurred just in season to make the great discovery of gold, through the immediate instrumentality of Marshall—who had found his way there from New Jersey—at the opportune moment when the title of the territory passed into our hands, free from any complication that might have arisen out of the more timely action of the English, the Mormons, or the raising of the Bear flag.

This precise and harmonious working of events to one great end, is worthy of more than a passing notice. It may well excite the interest and wonder of the human mind.

THE DISCOVERY OF GOLD BECOMES PUBLIC.

We left Sutter and Marshall examining the particles of gold and discussing the circumstances of the discovery. Marshall determined to return to the saw-mill—forty miles distant—that night, and he desired Captain Sutter to accompany him; but it was raining hard, and Captain Sutter concluded to remain till daylight. Marshall left immediately. In the morning Captain Sutter started for the saw-mill, and when within ten miles of that locality, he saw something coming out of the bushes by the road-side, a short distance in advance. At first he thought it was a grizzly bear, but it proved to be Marshall. Sutter inquired what he was doing there. Marshall replied that he had been to the saw-mill, and in his impatience he had returned thus far to meet him. They went on together, and on reaching the mill-race the laborers were found busily occupied picking up particles of gold.

After some examination, Captain Sutter became satisfied that gold in considerable quantities would be found in that neighborhood; and while the reflections of Marshall were probably confined to the idea of rapidly acquired wealth for himself, Captain Sutter realized at once how impossible it would be to hold his laborers to their work in carrying on his improvements, gathering his crops, and avoid being overrun by new-comers, should the gold prove abundant and the discovery be promulgated. He therefore begged the laborers to say nothing about the gold for six weeks. His grist-mill and some other improvements would then be completed, and his crops all gathered. The laborers promised to comply with his request, and Captain Sutter returned home on the 5th of February.

But the great secret could not long be retained. A bottle of whiskey made it known. A teamster whom Captain Sutter had dispatched to the saw-mill with supplies, heard of the discovery of gold, and managed to obtain some of the precious grains. On returning to the fort he immediately went to the neighboring store, kept by a Mormon, and demanded a bottle of whiskey. This was a cash article in that country, and as the teamster was poor pay, the trader refused to sell him the whiskey. The man declared he had plenty of money and exhibited some grains of gold. The astonished trader, on being satisfied that these were gold, gave his customer the bottle of whiskey, and earnestly inquired where he got the gold. The teamster refused to make known the secret till he had imbibed considerable of the liquor, when his tongue was loosened, and he told all about the discovery of gold at Sutter's saw-mill.

The wonderful tale spread like wild-fire throughout the sparsely inhabited Territory of California. It ran up and down the Pacific coast, traversed the continent, reached the Atlantic shores, and in a few months the story of California's golden treasures had startled the whole civilized world.

Many inaccurate and incomplete statements relative to this great discovery have been put forth. It has been published that a little daughter of Marshall first picked up pieces of gold in the saw-mill race and carried them to her father. This statement is entirely incorrect, as Marshall never had a daughter. He was not married then, and he lives a bachelor to this day.

It has also been published that a body of Mormons took out considerable gold on Mormon Island, Sacramento, in January, 1848. There is no truth in this statement. The diggings on Mormon Island were not discovered until some months after the discovery at Sutter's mill; and in fact, nothing had occurred in any part of California to detract from the credit or renown of the discovery now accorded to Marshall, the employé of Sutter.

CONSEQUENCES OF THE DISCOVERY TO MARSHALL.

But something yet remains to be told. The history and the romance of the great event would be incomplete should the two prominent figures in the foreground, Sutter and Marshall, be allowed to suddenly disappear, and their subsequent fortunes be consigned to oblivion.

The story of Marshall is simple and touching, as told by himself in documents which it is my good fortune to possess. From one of these, written in August, 1864, in which he sets forth his claim to a land-warrant, by virtue of his services in the Mexican War, I extract the following, *verbatim et literatim*. The document is valuable as a history of the trials and tribulations of Marshall, and as affording some insight into the condition of affairs in that region, immediately following the discovery of gold.

After speaking of building the saw-mill and discovering the gold, Marshall says: "We finished the mill and sawed a little lumber, when the valley poured in its inhabitants, each bent on gold. Then came the gold-fever. We could not employ the hands to run the mill. Thirteen of Sutter & Marshall's oxen soon went down into the cañons, thence down hungry men's throats. These cost $400 per yoke to replace. Seven of my horses went to carry weary men's packs. Sutter sold out to Bailey & Winter— we formed the firm of Bailey, Winter & Marshall, and before we could start the mill again, some white men murdered some Indians and ravished the squaws. The Indians retaliated, killed the men. A mob raised and started to hunt Indians, but could not find them. Took a second trip and found our friendly Indians; induced a part to come, telling them I wanted to talk to them; brought them to Coloma; picked out eight which were most friendly to me, and dismissed the others; drank plenty of whiskey; took out the eight Indians; placed them in the direction of our work-hands, whites and Indians; bid them run, commenced shooting, killed seven of the eight prisoners and one of my work-hands, an Indian. The mob threatened me to such an extent that my few friends advised me to leave for a season.

"Knowing the false manner that the Indians had been made to believe that I brought all the whites into the mountains, and had had their chief men murdered, I left until the mob dispersed, and the Indians could be made to know the truth. This was the commencement of my troubles. I will be brief with what remains.

"I returned, found a small town upon my settlement. I objected to these proceedings and was answered by some, 'No one wants your ground more than a year, then the mines will be worked out;' and by others, 'It is mineral land, you cannot preëmpt it, and we have as good a right to it as you.' I then could not believe that the circumstance of my finding gold was to deprive me of my rights of a settler and an American citizen, but such I soon found to be the case. I was soon forced to again leave Coloma for want of food. My property (that could be reached by a course of false litigation) was swept from me, and no one would give me employment. I have had to carry my pack of thirty or forty pounds over the mountains, living on China rice alone. If I sought employment, I was refused on the reasoning that I had discovered the gold-mines, and should be the one to employ them; they did not wish the man that made the discovery under their control. Again, should I commence mining upon old mining districts, I soon found some one claimed the ground, backed by a powerful mob who wanted to share the ground, believing that if I went to work there it was rich.

"Should I go to new localities, and commence to open a new mine, before I could prospect the ground numbers flocked in and commenced seeking all around me, and (as numbers tell) some one would find the lead before me and inform their party, and the ground was claimed; then I would travel again. Thus I wandered for more than four years. In the spring of 1857 I returned to Coloma, and was then able to get some work to do, such as digging gardens, sawing wood, clearing wells, etc. None would employ me at my trade to shove the plane and hand-saw. I next purchased some barren hills bordering on Coloma for fifteen dollars, and commenced planting a vineyard where I believe no one else would have attempted it, and I would not had I had the means to do better.

"Having given you a short history of myself and surroundings, I now, in few words, will tell and answer why I no sooner applied for my bounty-lands, feeling myself under some fatal influence, a curse, or at least some bad circumstances. I felt in my own mind that should I then call for my warrant, it would do me no good, and might be plucked from me. As these influences have gradually worn out, and now for some two years, since the fire of 1862, I find myself treated by those around me as they treat others, I have thought fit to apply for my land in hopes I may be able to raise the means to locate it in some healthy district, and by my labor procure me a couple of old nags to draw my plough (here I must do all by the spade), two or three cows, a few pigs and chickens, and end my few remaining days as comfortably as possible, being now fifty-four years old, having earned my land by faithful service. I see no reason why the Government should give to others and not to me. In God's name, can the circumstance of my being the first to find the gold regions of California be a cause to deprive me of every right pertaining to a citizen from under the flag? Little did my great-grandsire think that one of his descendants would have such feelings, when he set his name to the Articles of Independence (I mean the farmer from New Jersey).

"Hargraves from my advice returned to Australia, went into its mountains, and discovered gold, and was rewarded by being made wealthy by his government. I, who discovered gold in California, have been robbed of my all. How different has been our fortunes! he can bless the nation under whose flag he was born; should I curse mine?"

The following is an extract from one of Marshall's letters to General Bidwell, of California, on the occasion of his election to Congress:

"I hereby congratulate you on your success. I hope you may be able to render some assistance to General Sutter; he should be paid for losses sustained at breaking out of gold-fever. One thing appears to me remarkable, the persecution that has followed Sutter and myself, even when all was taken and we commenced making an effort to place ourselves in a comfortable situation as circumstances would allow, still retaining our papers as testimony of the past; the incendiary applies the torch to both our dwellings, all is destroyed. My cabin was destroyed in the fall of 1862, and all my papers went. Since then the persecution which followed me has in great measure ceased, and hope such will be the case with Sutter."

The simple and homely expressions of Marshall afford much valuable information. He evidently believed that a curse or something of an evil nature followed him for several years subsequent to the discovery of the gold. Misfortune was constantly in his path, and he suffered unjustly to the extent of his interest and enterprise, and though these were exceedingly limited as compared with Sutter's, they were every thing to him.

Through the exertions of the Hon. John Bidwell, Marshall obtained his soldier's land-warrant, but he still lives on his little farm near Coloma, and devotes himself to the culture of the finer quality of grapes, in which he has had marked success. He is somewhat prominent as a member of the California Agricultural Society, and it is said that he has recently become a convert to spiritualism.

Marshall is esteemed in his neighborhood as an honest, industrious, and good citizen, and there is every prospect that he will end his days in peace and comfort near the spot where, eighteen years ago, he discovered the gold.

CONSEQUENCES OF THE DISCOVERY TO SUTTER.

The consequences of the discovery of gold in California to the intelligent, large-hearted pioneer Sutter—him in whom centres the history of California for the last quarter of a century, cannot fail to be a matter of lively interest.

Frontier pioneers are made up of several classes. Some flee from society to escape the penalty of their crimes, others wander forth to escape the restraints of well-regulated society, while others go from pure love of adventure; and there are the unfortunate, the ruined, who seek to hide in the solitudes of Nature their mortification and their sorrows. But it is fair to presume that the mass of those who emigrate to new countries, to the wild frontier regions, are actuated by the spirit of enterprise, a desire to extend society and build up empire, believing that they can more readily create a home and do better for themselves generally in a new country than in the crowded haunts of men. Occasionally there stands out from this class one who, in intellect, breadth of conception, energy, courage, power to subjugate Nature, and true nobility of soul, towers above them all. Such was John A. Sutter.

This child of Nature, reared in the artificial society of Europe, was no reckless adventurer, seeking to escape the restraints of society, or to gratify an aimless love of roving and adventure. His whole history exhibits him as a man of broad, fixed, and intelligent purpose, and as pursuing this purpose with a single-mindedness seldom equalled.

We have read how Sutter, when a young man, liberally educated, having means and holding a good position in the army of France, cast his eyes across the broad Atlantic, and resolved to establish a colony of his countrymen—Swiss—on the frontiers of the United States, west of the Mississippi River. We have read how he came over to this country as the pioneer, and how at an early day his project was frustrated by disaster. With undaunted spirit and enlarged views, he conceives another plan—that of establishing a colony in the wilds of California. Several years are occupied in adventurous wandering, to reach the locality of his choice—that *terra incognita*, unexplored and unknown even to the intelligent inhabitants of the Territory of California. Once located, we find him casting his lot almost alone among the wild and barbarous tribes of Indians. Then we see him building a substantial fort on strictly military principles, mounting cannon, and bringing whites and savages under military disciplin. In a few years we find that he has subjugated the country around him, making friends of the wild and barbarous tribes of Indians, who at first were his fiercest enemies; and all this was accomplished, not more by his military tactics and resources, than by his powers of mind and attractive personal qualities in dealing with the rough, uncultivated whites and the wild children of Nature. Where once was found only the solitude, the silence, the desolation of isolated and unknown wilds, and where were heard the whoop and yell of savages, or the howl of wild beasts, there arose the habitations of civilized man. The ringing of the anvil, the sound of the hammer, the saw, and the plane, and the song of the husbandman, were heard. Broad fields teemed with the fruits of the earth, the plains were dotted with lowing herds, and peace and prosperity rested over the valley of the Sacramento.

The fame of this charming country and of its successful development by Sutter spread far and wide, and bands of emigrants began to turn their steps thither; and when any of these arrived, poor and destitute, their wants were bountifully and gratuitously supplied by the unselfish Sutter. *It is such as Sutter who are the real founders of empire.*

Even had there been no gold in California to discover, Sutter's enterprise would have forever stood out as the best conceived and most extensively successful instance of pioneering to be found in American history. But when it is connected with the fortuitous circumstances of the time, and the fact that it was through the direct agency of Sutter's enterprise that the gold was ultimately discovered, some years, doubtless, before it otherwise would have been, and that Sutter subjugated and partially peopled the country, by which the results of the great discovery were immensely hastened, it gives to the hero of the story a fame that can only be forgotten with the event itself.

At the time of the discovery of gold in California, February, 1848, it will be remembered that General Sutter was in peaceful and undisputed possession of immense tracts of land, of broad fields of growing crops, of a valuable military fort, of houses, shops, mills, and other improvements, and almost countless cattle, horses, sheep, and swine. He was the military commander of the district, and Indian agent of the territory. Respected and honored by all, General Sutter was the great man of the country. What is General Sutter's condition now? Let the following brief statement of facts answer:

A week after Sutter's return from the sawmill to the fort, February 5, 1848, the news of the discovery of the gold was generally known in that region, and, in consequence, he was immediately deserted by all his mechanics and laborers—white, Kanaka, and Indian. The mills were abandoned, and became a dead loss. Labor could not be hired to plant, to mature the crops, or reap and gather the grain that ripened.

At an early period subsequent to the discovery, an immense emigration from overland poured into the Sacramento Valley, making Sutter's domains their camping-ground, without the least regard for the rights of property. They occupied his cultivated fields, and squatted all over his available lands, saying they were the unappropriated domain of the United States, to which they had as good a right as any one. They stole and drove off his horses and mules, and exchanged or sold them in other parts of the country; they butchered his cattle, sheep, and hogs, and sold the meat. One party of five men, during the flood of 1849–'50, when the cattle were surrounded by water near the Sacramento River, killed and sold $60,000 worth of these—as it was estimated—and left for the States. By the first of January, 1852, the so-called settlers, under pretence of preëmption claims, had appropriated all Sutter's lands capable of settlement or appropriation, and they had stolen all his horses, mules, cattle, sheep, and hogs, except a small portion used and sold by himself.

There was no law to prevent this stupendous robbery; but when the law was established, there came lawyers with it to advocate the squatters' pretensions, although there were none from any part of Christendom who had not heard of Sutter's grants, the peaceful and just possession of which he had enjoyed for ten years, and his improvements were visible to all.

Sutter's efforts to maintain his rights, and save even enough of his property to give him an economical and comfortable living, constitute a sad history, one that would of itself fill a volume of painful interest. In these efforts he became involved in continuous and expensive litigation, which was not terminated till the final decision of the Supreme Court, in 1858–'59, a period of ten years.

When the United States Court of Land Commissioners was organized in California, Sutter's grants came up in due course for confirmation. These were the grant of eleven leagues, known as New Helvetia, and the grant of twenty-two leagues, known as the *Sobrante*.

The land commissioners found these grants perfect. Not a flaw or defect could be discoverd in either of them, and they were confirmed by the board, under the provisions of the treaty of Guadalupe Hidalgo.

The squatter interest then appealed to the United States District Court for the Northern District of California. This court confirmed the decision of the land commissioners. Extraordinary as it may appear, the squatter interest then appealed both cases to the Supreme Court of the United States, at Washington, and still more extraordinary to relate, that court, though it confirmed the eleven-league grant, decided that of the *Sobrante*—twenty-two leagues—in favor of the squatters. The court acknowledged that the grant was a "genuine and meritorious" one, and then decided in favor of the squatter interest on purely technical grounds, and Sutter's ruin was complete. This is one of the most singular cases of law *versus* justice that can be found in the annals of jurisprudence; and it shows very clearly that the science of law, as yet, is not, in reality, regulated by any standard above that which the low and selfish instincts of man have established.

The method of Sutter's ruin may be thus stated. He had been subjected to a very great outlay of money in the maintenance of his title, the occupancy and the improvement of the grant of New Helvetia.

From a mass of interesting documents which I have been permitted to examine, I obtained the following statement relative to the expenses incurred on that grant:

Expenses in money, and services, which formed the original consideration of the grant,	$50,000
Surveys and taxes on the same,	50,000
Cost of litigation extending through ten years, including fees to eminent counsel, witness fees, travelling expenses, etc.,	125,000
Amount paid out to make good the covenants of deeds upon the grant, over and above what was received from sales,	100,000
	$325,000

In addition, General Sutter had given titles to much of the *Sobrante* grant, under deeds of general warranty, which, after the decision of the Supreme Court of the United States in favor of the squatter interest, Sutter was obliged to make good, at an immense sacrifice, out of the New Helvetia grant; so that the confirmation of his title to this grant was, comparatively, of little advantage to him. Thus Sutter lost all his landed estate.

But amid the wreck and ruin that came

upon him in cumulative degree from year to year, Sutter managed to save, for a period, what is known as Hock farm, a very extensive and valuable estate on the Feather River. This estate he proposed to secure as a resting-place in his old age, and for the separate benefit of his wife and children, whom he had brought from Switzerland in 1852, having been separated from them eighteen years. Sutter's titles being generally discredited, his vast flocks and herds having dwindled to a few head, and his resources all gone, he was no longer able to hire labor to work the farm; and as a final catastrophe, the farm mansion was totally destroyed by fire in 1865, and with it all General Sutter's valuable records of his pioneer life.

As difficulties augmented, Sutter was obliged to trench on Hock Farm for the means of subsistence. His wife united with him in mortgage after mortgage on the farm, every foot of which, save one small piece, has long since been sold by the sheriff. That small piece is now at the mercy of the last mortgagee, and Sutter, with his family—he who, if allowed his rights, could buy out a Rothschild, an Astor, or a Stewart—

is absolutely a wanderer on the face of the earth, without a home or resting-place.

What a sad termination of a useful, noble, grand life—a life, the progressive results of which are felt, in a revolutionary degree, to the ends of the earth. The mind of man never conceived a fiction so strange as the truth of the story contained in this little book. The wildest dreams of the romancer never equalled the reality of this great romance of the age.

It seems incredible that the rich and great State of California, the generous instincts and liberal views of whose people never allow them to do any thing of a patriotic, honorable, and just character, on a small scale, can see their great pioneer pass from earth, unknown, unhonored, and in want; and it is still more incredible that the American nation can suffer so foul a blot on its escutcheon, as would be the historical fact, that the sun which illumined a life so genial and good—a life that has yielded, through hardship, toil, and courageous exposure, such immense national benefit—was permitted to go down in penury, sorrow, and gloom.

Any of these Books sent free by mail to any address on receipt of price.

RECENT PUBLICATIONS

OF

D. APPLETON & CO.,

443 and 445 Broadway, New York.

Haydn's Dictionary of Dates, re-

lating to all Ages and Nations, for Universal Reference; Comprehending Remarkable Occurrences, Ancient and Modern; the Foundation, Laws, and Government of Countries; their Progress in Civilization, Industry, Literature, Arts, and Science; their Achievements in Arms; their Civil, Military, and Religious Institutions, and particularly of the British Empire. By JOSEPH HADYN. Twelfth edition, greatly enlarged, and corrected to February, 1866. By BENJAMIN VINCENT. 1 vol., large 8vo, 833 pages, cloth. Price $7.50.

"Fifteen thousand articles all studded with facts as thick as the currants in a Christmas pudding."—*London Times.*

The World Before the Deluge.

By LOUIS FIGUIER. Containing 25 ideal landscapes of the ancient world, designed by Riou, and 208 figures of animals, plants, and other fossil remains and restorations. Translated from the Fourth French Edition. 1 vol. 8vo, 448 pages. $7.50.

"This work is written in the most entertaining manner. It unfolds the history of the world as shown in geology, from its supposed gaseous state until the era of the Noachian Deluge. * * * It is a good book, and good books are the need of the day."—*New York Commercial Advertiser.*

"No intelligent reader, caring aught for a knowledge of the construction of the globe on which he lives, can take this delightful volume into his hands with any cause for wonder that it has passed through four editions and found twenty-five thousand purchasers in less than two years—a demand, as the translator says, 'perhaps unprecedented for works of a scientific character.' But let no general reader be deterred from taking it by the fact that it is a 'scientific work.' It is written in the plainest and simplest language possible for the elucidation of its subject.—*New York Commissionaire.*"

The Harvest of the Sea. A Contribution to the Natural and Economic History of the British Food Fishes. By JAMES G. BERTRAM. With 50 illustrations. One large vol. 8vo, 520 pages. Cloth. Price $7.50.

"This is the first work in which an attempt has been made to bring before the public in one view the present position and future prospects of the Food Fishes. Great pains have been taken to obtain reliable information and correct statistics."—*Editor's Note.*

"Contains a large amount of highly interesting information and curious matter."—*The Athenæum.*

"For beauty of illustration, excellence of workmanship, and instructiveness of contents, has not been surpassed by any similar work lately issued."—*New York Times.*

The Works of Lord Macaulay

Complete. Edited by his sister, Lady TREVELYAN. With Portrait, engraved on steel, by W. Hull. 8 vols. large 8vo, cloth. Price $40; half calf extra, $56.

In preparing for publication a complete and uniform edition of Lord Macaulay's works, it has been thought right to include some portion of what he placed on record as a jurist in the East. The papers selected are the Introductory Report upon the Indian Penal Code, and the notes appended to that Code, in which most of its leading provisions were explained and defended. These papers were entirely written by Lord Macaulay.

The contents are arranged in this edition as follows: Vols. I. to IV., History of England since the Accession of James the Second; Vols. V., VI, and VII., Critical and Historical Essays, Biographies, Report and Notes on the Indian Penal Code, and contributions to Knight's Quarterly Magazine; Vol. VIII., Speeches, Lays of Ancient Rome, and Miscellaneous Poems.

A Treatise on the Steam-Engine

in its Various Applications to Mines, Mills, Steam Navigation, Railways, and Agriculture, with Theoretical Investigations respecting the Motive Power of Heat and the proper proportions of Steam-Engines, Elaborate Tables of the Right Dimensions of every part, and Practical Instructions for the Manufacture and Management of every species of Engine in Actual Use. By JOHN BOURNE. Being the Seventh Edition of "A Treatise on the Steam-Engine," by the "Artisan Club." Illustrated by 37 plates and 546 woodcuts. 1 vol. 4to, cloth. Price $18.00.

"The author is well known as an accomplished engineer; what he says will be accepted as truth."—*New York Commercial Advertiser.*

"The eminence of the author in his profession makes this work authority on the subjects of which it treats."—*Eastern Argus.*

Homes Without Hands, being a

description of the habitations of animals, classed according to their principles of construction. By the Rev. J. G. WOOD, M. A. F. L. S., author of the "Illustrated Natural History," etc., with new designs by W. E. Keyl and E. Smith. Engraved by G. Pearson. 1 vol. large 8vo, 21 full-page drawings and 85 illustrations; 632 pages. Cloth. Price $7.50.

"One of the most charming Natural History books we have ever read."—*Glasgow Herald.*

"A clever original work on Natural History, which is certain to take its place among permanent literature."—*Globe.*

"A really more instructive and entertaining work on Natural History has not been published."—*Leeds Intelligencer.*

"'Homes Without Hands' is one of the most interesting and instructive works on Natural History."—*Observer.*

"No volume lately published contains so much curious and interesting information, presented in so attractive a form, as Mr. Wood's work, which he has aptly and happily named 'Homes Without Hands.'"—*New York Times.*

Mythology of Ancient Greece

and Italy. By THOMAS KEIGHTLEY, author of "The History of Greece," "The History of Rome," "Fairy Mythology," "Tales and Popular Fictions," etc. Third edition. Revised and augmented. With 12 plates from the antique. 1 vol., large 8vo, 512 pages, cloth. Price $6.00.

This work has reached its third edition, and has been carefully revised, and has received numerous additions. Mr. Pococke, in his late work, terms it "the best compendium of Hellenic mythology that has appeared, and will always deservedly maintain its high position as the exponent of what the Greeks thought and wrote about and believed."

The Horse. By WM. YOUATT.

With a Treatise on Draught. Revised and enlarged. By WALKER WATSON, M. R. C. V. S. With numerous illustrations. 1 vol. 8vo, 589 pages. Price, cloth, $4.00.

"* * * The present edition will be found to have undergone a thorough revision and arrangement, many fresh diseases have been introduced, and the nature and treatment of others considered in accordance with the principles of veterinary science at the present day."

"This is an excellent and comprehensive work on the subject of which it treats."—*Philadelphia Inquirer.*

"We hope every lover and owner of a horse will secure a copy, and learn how to treat the faithful beast."—*Troy Times.*

The Treasury of Bible Knowledge.

Being a Dictionary of the Books, Persons, Places, Events, and other Matters of which Mention is made in Holy Scripture. Intended to establish its Authority and Illustrate its Contents. By Rev. JOHN AYRE, M. A., of Gonville and Caius College, Cambridge. With 15 full-page engravings, 5 colored maps, and many hundred woodcuts. 1 vol., thick 18mo, 944 pages, cloth. Price $5.

"The best of the new books. * * * We know of none more valuable than 'The Treasury of Bible Knowledge.' It is in all respects the best, as it is the most convenient manual for the Biblical student yet published. Especial attention has been given to the clear and full presentation of the evidence of Christianity, and the latest and most complete arguments in regard to the authenticity and inspiration of the various books of the Bible."—*American Baptist.*

"* * * One of the most valuable publications ever issued by that house. In fact, the book may be pronounced an Encyclopædia or Library of Scriptural Information."—*New Yorker.*

A Smaller Classical Dictionary

of Biography, Mythology, and Geography. By WILLIAM SMITH, LL.D., Editor of the Dictionaries of "Greek and Roman Antiquities," "Biography and Mythology, etc. Abridged from the larger Dictionary. Illustrated by 200 engravings on wood. 1 vol. 12mo, 464 pages, cloth. Price $3.00.

"It will fill admirably a want heretofore much felt in school and classical literature."—*New Yorker.*

"It will be found a very desirable work for students."—*New York Commercial Advertiser.*

The Old Testament History.

From the Creation to the return of the Jews from Captivity. Edited by WILLIAM SMITH, LL.D., with 10 maps and numerous woodcuts. 619 pages. 1 vol. 12mo, cloth. Price $3.00.

"* * * Besides giving the history recorded in the Old Testament, with the necessary explanations, notes, references, and citations, this work contains information on a large number of other subjects. Among these may be mentioned an account of each of the Books of the Bible, the geography of the Holy Land and of other countries, together with the political and ecclesiastical antiquities of the Jews, Historical and Genealogical Tables, etc."—*Extract from Preface.*

A Complete Biblical Library.

THE
TREASURY OF BIBLE KNOWLEDGE:
BEING
A DICTIONARY
OF

The Books, Persons, Places, Events, and other matters, of which mention is made in Holy Scripture. Intended to establish its authority and illustrate its contents.

By REV. JOHN AYRE, M. A.,
OF GONVILLE AND CAIUS COLLEGE, CAMBRIDGE.

Illustrated with many hundred woodcuts and fifteen full-page steel plates, drawn by Justyne, from original photographs by Graham, and five colored maps. 1 thick volume, 12mo, 944 pages. Price, Cloth, $5.00; Half Calf, $6.50.

Sent free by mail on receipt of the price.

"The general object of this work is to promote the intelligent use of the Sacred Volume by furnishing a mass of information respecting Palestine, and the manners, customs, religion, literature, arts, and attainments of the inhabitants; an account of the countries and races with which the Hebrews had relations, together with some notice of all the persons and places mentioned in the Bible and Apocrypha. The history and authority of the books themselves are discussed conjointly and severally. I have been anxious to study the best authorities for what is asserted, and to bring up the information to the most modern standard. I have not written hastily, therefore, but have spent some years in the compilation of this volume."—*Extract from the Preface.*

"Among the books which should find a place in the collection of every Christian man, who seeks to have in his possession any thing beyond a Bible and hymn-book, we know of none more valuable than 'The Treasury of Bible Knowledge.' It is in all respects the best, as it is the most convenient manual for the Biblical student yet published. We hope to see this work in the hands of every Sunday-school and Bible-class teacher."—*American Baptist.*

"* * * One of the most valuable publications ever issued by that house."—*New Yorker.*

D. APPLETON & COMPANY,
Publishers and Booksellers,
443 & 445 Broadway, New York.

D. APPLETON & CO.'S PUBLICATIONS.

THE ONLY COMPLETE AND UNIFORM EDITION.

LORD MACAULAY'S WORKS,

EDITED BY HIS SISTER,

LADY TREVELYAN.

8 Vols., large 8vo. Price, cloth, $40.00; half calf extra, $56.00; full calf extra, $64.00. Beautifully printed in large clear type, on thick toned paper, with a fine portrait engraved on steel by W. Holl.

In preparing for publication a complete and uniform edition of Lord Macaulay's Works, it has been thought right to include some portion of what he placed on record as a jurist in the East. The papers selected are the Introductory Report on the Indian Penal Code, and the Notes appended to that code, in which most of its leading provisions were explained and defended. These papers were entirely written by Lord Macaulay, but the substance of them was the result of the joint deliberations of the Indian Law Commission, of which he was President. They are by no means merely of Indian interest, for while they were the commencement of a new system of law for India, they relate chiefly to general principles of jurisprudence, which are of universal application.

The contents are arranged in this edition as follows: Vols. I. to IV., History of England since the Accession of James the Second; Vols. V., VI., and VII., Critical and Historical Essays, Biographies, Report and Notes on the Indian Penal Code, and contributions to Knight's Quarterly Magazine; Vol. VIII., Speeches, Lays of Ancient Rome, and Miscellaneous Poems.

This last division of the work is completed by the insertion of the Cavalier's Song and the Poetical Valentine to the Hon. Mary C. Stanhope, two pieces which were not included in previous editions of Lord Macaulay's miscellaneous writings.

"Every admirer of Lord Macaulay's writings (and their name is legion) will heartily thank Appleton & Co. for having produced this elegant edition of his works. It seems almost idle to say any thing in praise of the great historian to the American reader, but we cannot forbear expressing our admiration of the physical as well as mental strength so manifest in his diction and style. . . . . But it is not our intention to write a critique on the man whose memory holds so prominent a place in the heart of the reading world. The volumes before us should fill a niche in every public and private library in our land."—*Glen Falls Journal.*

"His writings and his speeches, arranged in chronological order, exhibit the developments of a mind always more or less powerful, and announce the extent of his reading and the tenacity of his memory. His contributions to the History of British India show how usefully his time was spent during his sojourn at Calcutta."

☞ D. Appleton & Co.'s Descriptive Catalogue may be had gratuitously on application.

D. APPLETON & CO.,

Publishers, Booksellers, & Stationers,

443 & 445 Broadway, N. Y.

POPULAR NOVELS,

BY CELEBRATED AUTHORS.

The Select Library of Fiction.

THE BEST, CHEAPEST, AND MOST POPULAR NOVELS PUBLISHED, WELL PRINTED IN CLEAR, READABLE TYPE, ON GOOD PAPER, AND STRONGLY BOUND.

The Hunchback of Notre-Dame. By VICTOR HUGO, Author of "Les Misérables," etc. 1 vol., 12mo. Fancy paper covers, $1.00; cloth, $1.25.

Doctor Thorne. By ANTHONY TROLLOPE, Author of "Orley Farm," "Can You Forgive Her," etc. 1 vol., 12mo. Fancy paper covers, $1.00; cloth, $1.25.

The Jealous Wife. By MISS PARDOE, Author of "Rival Beauties," etc. 1 vol., 12mo. Fancy paper covers, $1.00; cloth, $1.25.

Tilbury Nogo; or, Passages in the Life of an Unsuccessful Man. By WHYTE MELVILLE, Author of "Digby Grand," etc., etc. 1 vol., 12mo. Fancy paper covers, $1.00; cloth, $1.25.

Harry Lorrequer. By CHARLES LEVER, Author of "Charles O'Malley," etc. 1 vol., 12mo. Fancy paper covers, $1.00; cloth, $1.25.

The Ogilvies. By MISS MULOCK, Author of "John Halifax, Gentleman," etc. 1 vol., 12mo. Fancy paper covers, $1.00; cloth, $1.25.

Ruth. By MRS. GASKELL, Author of "Wives and Daughters," "Mary Barton," etc. 1 vol., 12mo. Fancy paper covers, $1.00; cloth, $1.25.

The Head of the Family. By MISS MULOCK, Author of "Olive," "Agatha's Husband," etc. 1 vol., 12mo. Fancy paper covers, $1.00; cloth, $1.25.

Lindisfarn Chase. By THOMAS A. TROLLOPE, Author of "Beppo," etc. 1 vol., 12mo. Fancy paper covers, $1.00; cloth, $1.25.

Olive. By MISS MULOCK, Author of "The Head of the Family," "The Ogilvies." 1 vol., 12mo. Fancy paper covers, $1.00; cloth, $1.25.

Mary Barton. By MRS. GASKELL, Author of "Ruth," etc., etc. 1 vol., 12mo. Fancy paper covers, $1.00; cloth, $1.25.

Agatha's Husband. By MISS MULOCK, Author of "John Halifax, Gentleman." 1 vol., 12mo. Fancy paper covers, $1.00; cloth, $1.25.

Either of the above sent free by mail on receipt of the price.

D. APPLETON & COMPANY,

Booksellers, Publishers, and Stationers,

443 & 445 Broadway, New York.

The most attractive Gift Book ever published.
Ready on the First of October.

THE LIFE OF MAN SYMBOLIZED
BY
THE MONTHS OF THE YEAR,
In their Seasons and Phases, with Passages selected from Ancient and Modern Authors,
BY RICHARD PIGOTT.

Accompanied by a series of Twenty-five full-page Illustrations, and many hundred Marginal Devices, Decorated Initial Letters and Tail-pieces, engraved on Wood from Original Designs, by JOHN LEIGHTON.

Half Morocco Extra, $20; Full Morocco Extra, or Antique, $25; Super Extra Bindings, from $30 to $45.

This volume consists of Twelve Sections, into which the Life of Man is divided, to accord with the Twelve Months of the Year, and the progress of nature, from the germination of the seed to the decay of the tree.

The progressive developments of the physical and moral attributes of Man are shown in each Month concurrently with the growth of the Year; and the varying phases of his passions, pursuits, and aspirations are exhibited in passages taken from ancient and modern writers. These are cited in the typographical characters of their respective periods, appropriately and suggestively illustrated by many hundreds of marginal devices, initial vignettes, and tail-pieces.

Each page of the book is enclosed in a framework, which serves as a setting for proverbs, and other aphorismatic sentences, in harmony with the text. Each section is preceded by two full-page engravings, of which, including the general frontispiece, there are twenty-five, printed within red rules. Twelve of them, illustrating the life of man from the cradle to the grave, also embody the progress of the seasons, and the varying aspects of nature, as seen under an English sky. The other twelve comprise a series of medallion portraits, from the infant to the patriarch, combined with floral emblems and other symbolical attributes, in keeping with the central subject.

Subjects of the Thirteen Cardinal Illustrations:

Frontispiece.—All the World's a Stage.

THE INFANT.
January.—The Birth of the Year. The tender offspring is rescued from the snow. The scion parted from the parent tree.

THE SCHOOLBOY.
February.—Train up a child in the way he should go. As the sapling is pruned and bent, so will it grow.

THE STRIPLING.
March.—Mental and physical exercises combine to develop the youthful faculties. The supple tree bends to the breeze, buds, and strengthens.

THE LOVER.
April.—Love and hope temper and teach the early man—as the tree develops under sunshine and shower.

THE FATHER.
May.—The man becomes the father of many children—as the tree extends its branches and puts forth fruitful buds.

THE SOLDIER.
June.—With increased strength come greater trials and duties—as the tree grows, more stoutly does it resist the elements.

THE MERCHANT.
July.—The mind sobers with age. Gravity and prudence mark the man. The laden tree is less agitated by every gentle breeze.

THE MAGISTRATE.
August.—The pursuits of an industrious, useful life tend to a peaceful rest—as the fruitful tree reposes whilst yet clothed with verdure.

THE PHILOSOPHER.
September.—Man is borne onward. Wisdom and charity are the solace of his declining years. The tree reposes after filling the garner with its fruit.

THE GRANDSIRE.
October.—Infirmities steal on. A man's actions form precedents for his grandchildren.—As the tree decays, it enriches the soil for a future generation.

THE CENSOR.
November.—The senses grow dim, and strength gradually fails. The venerable tree, unable longer to support itself, requires aid.

THE PATRIARCH.
December.—The flame of life departs from the body, the spirit flies,—as the withered trunk is prostrated before the gale.

D. Appleton & Co., 443 & 445 Broadway, N. Y.

STATIONERY.

D. APPLETON & CO.,
IMPORT STATIONERS,
443 & 445 BROADWAY, NEW YORK.

STATIONERY, FOREIGN AND DOMESTIC,
In all its Branches.

BLANK BOOKS,
OF ALL DESCRIPTIONS, FROM STOCK OR MADE TO ORDER.

FRENCH PAPERS,
From the Celebrated D'Angouleme Mills.

ALEX. PIRIE & SON'S
EXTRA SUPERFINE NOTE PAPERS AND ENVELOPES.

Initial Stamping Presses and Dies,
For Colored and Plain Stamping.

PARKER'S TREASURY BLOTTING,
60, 80, 100, and 120 pounds, both White and Colored.

ARNOLD'S FLUID AND COPYING INK.
GUYOT'S FRENCH VIOLET COPYING INK.
Whatman's Drawing Papers.
ENGLISH ROLL DRAWING PAPERS.—DITTO MOUNTED ON CLOTH.

REYNOLDS & SONS' BRISTOL BOARDS.
Visiting Cards. Wedding Envelopes.
MONOGRAMS Designed and Engraved in the Best Style of the Art.

MOURNING STATIONERY,
Cards, Paper, and Envelopes, in any width of Border required.

D. APPLETON & CO.'S PUBLICATIONS.

A STANDARD BOOK OF REFERENCE.

THE
HOUSEHOLD BOOK OF POETRY.

Collected and Edited by CHARLES A. DANA.

Tenth Edition. Royal 8vo. 798 pp. Beautifully printed.

Half mor., gilt top, $; half calf, extra, $; mor. ant., $.

"The purpose of this book is to comprise within the bounds of a single volume whatever is truly beautiful and admirable among the minor poems of the English language. * * * Especial care has also been taken to give every poem entire and unmutilated, as well as in the most authentic form which could be procured."
—*Extract from Preface.*

"This work is an immense improvement on all its predecessors. The editor, who is one of the most erudite of scholars, and a man of excellent taste, has arranged his selections under ten heads, namely: Poems of Nature, of Childhood, of Friendship, of Love, of Ambition, of Comedy, of Tragedy and Sorrow, of the Imagination, of Sentiment and Reflection, and of Religion. The entire number of poems given is about two thousand, taken from the writings of English and American poets, and including some of the finest versions of poems from ancient and modern languages. The selections appear to be admirably made, nor do we think that it would be possible for any one to improve upon this collection."—*Boston Traveller.*

"Within a similar compass, there is no collection of poetry in the language that equals this in variety, in richness of thought and expression, and of poetic imagery."—*Worcester Palladium.*

"This is a choice collection of the finest poems in the English language, and supplies in some measure the place of an extensive library. Mr. Dana has done a capital service in bringing within the reach of all the richest thoughts that grace our standard poetical literature."—*Chicago Press.*

"A work that has long been required, and, we are convinced from the selections made, and the admirable manner in which they are arranged, will commend itself at once to the public."—*Detroit Advertiser.*

"Never was a book more appropriately named. By the exercise of a sound and skilful judgment, and a thorough familiarity with the poetical productions of all nations, the compiler of this work has succeeded in combining, within the space of a single volume, nearly every poem of established worth and compatible length in the English language."—*Philadelphia Journal.*

"It gives us in an elegant and compact form such a body of verse as can be found in no other volume or series of volumes. It is by far the most complete collection that has ever been made of English lyrical poetry."—*Boston Transcript.*

"Among the similar works which have appeared we do not hesitate to give this the highest place."—*Providence Journal.*

"We are acquainted with no selections which, in point of completeness and good taste, excel the 'Household Book of Poetry.'"—*Northwestern Home Journal.*

"It is almost needless to say that it is a mine of poetic wealth."—*Boston Post.*

www.ingramcontent.com/pod-product-compliance
Lightning Source LLC
Chambersburg PA
CBHW030347170426
43202CB00010B/1274